How Companies *Really* Grow

To: Derek Barker.
With Best Wishes
Ciaran Walsh.

How Companies *Really* Grow

Carpe diem, quam minimum credula postero
Seize the day, placing little trust in the future
(Horace: Odes, Book 1, xi)

Ciaran Walsh

Matador
5 Weir Road
Kibworth Beauchamp
Leicester LE8 0LQ, UK
Tel: (+44) 116 279 2299
Fax: (+44) 116 279 2277
Email: books@troubador.co.uk
Web: www.troubador.co.uk/matador

ISBN 978 1848765 825

British Library Cataloguing in Publication Data.
A catalogue record for this book is available from the British Library.

Typeset in 12pt Perpetua by Troubador Publishing Ltd, Leicester, UK

Matador is an imprint of Troubador Publishing Ltd

Printed in Great Britain by the MPG Books Group, Bodmin and King's Lynn

Acknowledgements

Many people have helped me in the task of writing this book. In particular, Andrea Defries, a business adviser colleague, initiated the project by suggesting that I should write a book based on my experience of advising hundreds of companies in relation to their growth. Other colleagues kept me going by giving me encouragement throughout the sometimes fraught writing task.

My thanks go to the critical readers who were incisive with their comments and kept me on the straight and narrow. I am indebted to Lesley Bees, Barbara Stevens, John Woolsey and Reg Illingworth for all their hard work.

Finally, I am grateful to the many client companies that contributed to my experience and knowledge in respect of how companies really grow.

Ciaran Walsh

Contents

Chapter 1

Black Holes

This book sets out the essential processes that you will need on the way to creating a successful company. You will need to progress through the Phases of Growth, bit by bit. These phases are set out in summary form below.

It is very strange that people who have written about the phases or stages of growth of companies seem to disappear, as if they had been sucked into a black hole and now only exist as a singularity. Nothing can escape the gravitational pull of a black hole, communications included, so we hear no more on the subject from these writers. About half a dozen writers have had a shot at explaining the chronological development of companies since the 1960s. The longest treatise on the subject is about 12 pages by Neil Churchill, a professor at Insead management school. So few pages do not allow for much detail, and headings with brief descriptions are inadequate to properly inform a manager as to the relevance of each phase or stage.

This book is somewhat longer and more detailed, and informs the manager, consultant or adviser how to manage and what to do in each phase. Growing a company implies that the founder has a future goal in mind. Here, I make the assumption that the company is aiming to make money for its shareholders, from both cash distribution from time to time and from capital growth as expressed in the value of the shares. This does not exclude a core belief such as aiming to have the happiest customers in the world.

There are other types of company where the goal of the owners may not be the creation of wealth, and yet other types of companies where growth is absent due to the intrinsic nature of the structure and *raison d'etre*, but the money-making machine is by far the most prevalent.

The nature of the company that this book applies to is the money-making machine. In essence, very distilled, it is a company that engages in a creative act and produces a product or service. It then hones that product to suit the market and replicates it over and over again. By way of note, for the rest of this book I will use the word 'product' to include services, since both are a product of the company, just as 4 is a product of 2 x 2.

Very little research is available on small and growing companies and what is available is of poor quality. This is not all that surprising, bearing in mind that large companies are where the money is; by which I mean the money to endow Chairs in Business Studies at universities and to fund projects that relate directly to the problems and opportunities of large companies.

A common methodology used by academics in researching small company matters is to send a student out to interview a dozen owners of small firms and attempt to draw conclusions from the result. Usually, the interviews last an hour or two and are based on a preconceived hypothesis. One report that I read concluded that marketing in small firms consisted only of making friends with the individual customers and subsequently selling to them. I think the sampling for that piece of research was a little skewed – it was probably conducted entirely on companies that performed as local builders' merchants, with their usual 40 main customers, all of whom play golf. This is an example of a genre of companies that get stuck in the Reactive Phase.

A professor of business at a university whose name I will omit to mention, concluded that the larger the branch of a franchise, the more capital was needed to start it up. In addition, he further concluded that the larger the retail premises, the greater the sales volume achieved. Stunning stuff!

One of the reasons why the available research is of such poor quality is that academics form hypotheses first and then attempt to prove or disprove them. Forming a hypothesis is effectively making an assumption. That assumption locks out all other information, as the questions asked are focused on the basis of the assumption and the answers are interpreted in the light of the assumption. Consequently, the results can yield only a tiny bit of information, and very often that information is mundane and sometimes entirely inaccurate. A further complication is that a student conducting the field research is unlikely to report back with a completely negative result – that the hypotheses cannot be proved or disproved – and is likely to be open to bias in interpreting the answers and results. Everybody likes a good story and the researcher will oblige. Newspapers do not print headlines saying 'NO NEWS TODAY'.

Another dreadful research method that has been frequently used is the postal questionnaire. The sampling is skewed because only some of the questionnaires are returned and those that do get sent back are self-selecting and may all express the same opinions, whereas the subjects who have not replied may all be of a different viewpoint. There is always the temptation to tell a little lie when filling in the answers on a printed questionnaire.

Entrepreneurs tend, when approached by relative strangers such as researchers, to be economical with the truth. Post hoc rationalisation will always make them cast their histories in a favourable light. Motivated by fear of embarrassment, they might even lie. Sometimes, they will engage in some wicked fun, deliberately misleading the research interviewer. Remember Margaret Mead and her book *Coming of Age in Samoa*, an anthropological study? Ms. Mead had made friends with two of her teenage subjects in Samoa who completely misled her, just for fun, and she believed every word and wrote it up in her book. The book was a standard academic text for years.

Subsequently, the misinformation was 'exposed' by Derek Freeman in his book. One of the key reasons was the methodology, especially the fact that Ms. Mead had spent eight months on her project whilst Freeman spent over three years researching in Samoa. And Mead believed what her subjects told her, just like entrepreneurs mislead researchers. To vindicate research on entrepreneurial behaviour one needs to be a 'fly-on-the-wall' and present from the start a decision process, through the implementation and in at the final result.

My research methodology is to disappear down into another type of black hole, one with a pithead and an elevator that takes me to one of the many coal faces at the end of the numerous tunnels. Anthropologists call it 'action research'. I call it getting down and dirty at the coal face, getting involved and working with the subjects in a practical way, being in the situation with them and being fully aware of the context in which thoughts and actions are taking place. Perceiving the whole process of decision making and knowing the state of mind of the decision maker makes for a more accurate picture.

Many of the books about small business are based on start-ups by now famous entrepreneurs. Nobody writes about the failures, only the successes, because few people have been working inside companies from start-up to failure. But I have seen both ends of the spectrum – and the bits in between, including the agonies, the depressions, the 'irrational' behaviour, the anger, the lack of staying power and all the diseases that a small company can suffer from. And there is much to be learned here; preventing failures is as important as identifying growth opportunities.

One of the intrinsic difficulties of the usual methods of research is that they deal only with explicit knowledge, whereas the implicit knowledge is very important. Some of the methods used in writing to transfer tacit knowledge include the use of metaphors, analogies and similes. One analogy on its own may not be sufficient, since analogies are not the knowledge that one wants to impart, just an aspect of it, a partial truth. To explain a concept, sometimes multiple analogies and metaphors are needed. The transmitter of the knowledge must beware of premature closure, leaving the recipient with an unbalanced view of the concept. The problem with a book is that there is no immediate feedback from the reader to the author, and the author must assume that the readers' reactions are all similar to the reactions of the critical readers on which the book has been tested. You will find many analogies and metaphors in play in this book, being my devices for transferring tacit knowledge to you, the reader.

The book that I write is for use not only by entrepreneurs about to start up, but by owner managers of small companies that may be well established. Although I use the format of addressing the entrepreneur throughout, it is also written for those who advise the managers in small companies. It will be helpful to consultants, accountants and bankers and, of course, their clients. Anyone with an interest in small companies such as stockbrokers, solicitors, venture capital providers and business angels will derive considerable benefit from this book.

There is a third black hole, one into which advisers of small companies frequently fall – the holistic hole. Intervening in a company and making changes to some functional parts, without knowing and considering the effect on the whole, is dangerous. When functions get out of sync, it can lead to the failure of a company. Consultants and other advisers need to know the phase of growth that a small, growing company has reached; otherwise they will approach when the company is not yet ready for their advice or when it is too late and, even worse, they might advise inappropriately. Mistiming of advice is very common and is very confusing to the entrepreneur.

Companies grow not by discrete stages with a clear cut beginning and end, but through 'phases'. Phases arrive at appropriate times in the development of a company and sometimes they overlap. They do not have finite endings and, once experienced, there will be frequent regressions as changes are undertaken by the managers. Once you hire a person you have not completed hiring – you have to do it repeatedly through the lifetime of a company. The phases of growth that I describe are different to the stages of growth models that have gone before, and I would claim that they are more precise, more practical to understand and put to use, and more detailed.

My names for the phases of growth are more descriptive and, to further help with remembering them, they form an acronym. CARPE DIEM is an acronym for

Creative, Analysis, Reactive, Processes, Empowerment and Divisions in Extended Markets. Believe me, I didn't start out trying to fit the names of the phases to a preconceived acronym, apt as it is – it just happened. I admit only to changing 'Delegation', my original name, to 'Empowerment' and 'Systems' to 'Processes' when I spotted the pattern emerging. It was just like starting a company. After you start you begin to observe patterns that are meaningful only after you have started.

- The Creative Phase is when and how you devise the business idea.
- The Analysis Phase is where you collect enough information to ensure that your idea will work as you intend it to do.
- The Reactive Phase is where start to sell your product and react to the feedback from your customers.
- The Processes Phase comes when you are achieving the necessary sales and making profits.
- The Empowerment Phase comes with growth and is the time when you need to delegate the processes to others.
- The Divisions Phase is when you can create and separate divisions that differ from your main business.

Many small, growing companies try to carry out inappropriate activities at the wrong phase of growth. Many cramp their behaviour, in the Analysis Phase, by producing huge and elaborate plans for five years ahead. In the Reactive Phase, some decide that they will launch several different products at the same time and end up very confused.

Some try to delegate too early to their employees, consequently losing momentum and the drive that only the boss can inject. Some have inadequate processes in place at the beginning, whilst others are stifled by too many as they start up. Frequently, I encounter companies that are trying to run several businesses as if they were one, unaware of the Divisions Phase. Problems arise when the managers of the company do not know what to do at each phase of growth, because they are not conscious that the Phases of Growth exist. Those problems that arise from not understanding the Phases of Growth and taking them into account are major inhibitors of growth.

Each phase follows on from the previous one in a logical manner and each phase adds lots of learning and lots of strength to the body corporate, all of which is necessary to cope with the future phases. Do not rush through the phases and do not leave one out; if you do, you will regret it later. The Phases of Growth are sometimes described as a 'natural' progression and the analogy commonly used is based on human growth phases. This analogy should be used sparingly. The phases of growth in companies are not natural because companies are not organic forms, and moving on to the next phase can be resisted quite easily. It requires a decision and a positive effort to move a company on to the next phase.

Knowing what the phases are and what they involve, and knowing the order in which they arrive, makes running a business a whole lot easier and less stressful. You can then intentionally drive through the Phases of Growth, ignoring what the less informed will perceive as serious problems and concentrating on the activities relevant to the phase you are in. Knowing what to ignore is a very powerful element of knowledge, so use it. A sailing analogy works well. In the Creative Phase you are deciding what port you are heading for and in the Analysis Phase you are sorting out your charts and tide times and checking the weather forecasts. Then you launch into the Reactive Phase, putting the spinnaker up, making the fastest speed you can, and reacting to the wind, the sea and the weather. GPS is needed here, to constantly ascertain your position. As you reach calmer seas, well on your way, you enter the Processes Phase. You drop the spinnaker, get your compass out, set your course and tie the tiller down – it is plain sailing now. Then you, the skipper, go below to dream of future destinations, delegating command of the boat to your first mate, as you enter the Empowerment Phase. You arrive at your destination port and then consider where else you might go. Whilst sailing from Southampton in the UK to the Hamptons in Connecticut, you have realised that you now know how to sail to the Caribbean or Maine. So you can now start another venture – the Divisions Phase can be entered.

Setting up your own business is perceived as being very risky. None of the business owners that I have encountered had been trained to run a real business. It is my hope that, having read this book, you will increase your knowledge and thereby reduce the risk considerably.

A word for advisers to small business owners: people who start their own companies are rational human beings. If you observe apparently irrational behaviour, it probably means that you do not really know what's going on. I hope this book will help you to identify the rationality of some of this behaviour.

A public relations firm achieved rapid growth over the first few years of its life. It now employed about 20 people. However, during the last year the sales revenue remained static, as did the number of employees. When I met with the directors they had considerable difficulty in expressing the nature of their problems. Firstly, they were of the opinion that the employees were not sufficiently committed to their jobs, but they could not define what they meant by that. When I asked what they wanted for the future of the company, they floundered, "We want to be the best P.R. agency", they said. "What does the best mean, exactly?" I asked. They fluffed and floundered more.

What had happened was that they had reached the end of the Reactive Phase of growth of the company. They needed to change in order to grow further, but they could not define the problems, or the solutions – it all just seemed to be messy and unsatisfactory. The solution was to enter the Processes Phase and formalise their successful systems, thereby enabling them to enter the Empowerment Phase and delegate processes to others.

The name of this book and the names of the phases are meant to be memorable, based on my assumption that most people read a book only once. However, I strongly recommend that you read this book more than once and keep it by you as a reference for when you find yourself stuck. As you read through you will see that I make comments relating to future phases. The implications of these comments may not be fully appreciated unless you read through again.

Section I

Creative Phase

Chapter 2

How Businesses Really Start

Has it occurred to you that the business world is completely full, so much so that there is absolutely no room whatsoever for another business? Some academic writers have decided that it really is full. To quote from an MBA textbook: "There are no cosy niches in the business world, nowhere to hide from the competition" However, you are now reading a book that you have never read before and that has never been available on the market before. It is a new product and it exists and thrives within its own niche, different from the niche that romantic novels nestle within. You have bought a new product, one that is different from all other products in some way that, hopefully, you will find of value to you.

The statement, "There are no cosy niches in the business world..." implies that the world has now stopped and that it is replete with businesses. The writer of the MBA textbook is suffering from a disease known as 'industrialitis', which presents as an uncontrollable need to categorise businesses into industry types. Industry categories were invented many years ago by civil servants who had the job of managing the macro-economy of the country. As you know, civil servants need to collect statistics in order to produce a rationalisation to justify why their policies have gone wrong. Industry definitions of just a few years ago have now blurred and have merged into each other. Computers, telephones, television, cinemas and printing have collided and meshed. The boundaries of all 'industries' are so blurred that for practical purposes it is useless to refer to them. You could say that there is no such thing as an industry or that every discrete economic activity is an industry in itself.

There is a never-ending stream of new companies being created, producing a never-ending river of new and modified products, running into an ever-changing ocean of customers. Many of these new, and consequently small, companies have created an 'industry' just for themselves, different from other companies in some significant way. They have created or spotted niches that are very cosy indeed and they are still doing it today. Many of these companies are very successful and hopefully, having read this book, you will feel confident enough to create your own company within its very own cosy niche. Or several cosy niches. During the course of this book I will refer to many such successful companies – and some unsuccessful ones.

The world is always in a state of flux, always changing and, as might be expected, all change introduces new opportunities. For example, changes in technological hardware are easy to spot because they are tangible, observable and touchable. But many other things change over time, sometimes quickly, sometimes slowly. Language is always changing, apparent from the difference in English from Shakespeare's day to now. New words and phrases are constantly being introduced in order to express new concepts and ideas. The language we use changes to accommodate changes in behaviour. If the new words communicate attractive ideas, behaviours change to accommodate these new words. Not many people, except for Italians, would have used expressions like *Caffe Latte, Capuccino* or *espresso* even 30 years ago. These expressions are now commonplace and consequently people behave differently. Travelling to work in large cities, commuters are frequently accompanied by a Capuccino, a practice unheard of a generation ago.

Clone Zone, a retail company, was founded during the 1970s to address the needs and desires of the gay community. The opportunity it exploited was a sociological change, in that greater tolerance of gayness had become a feature of our society at that time. The law had been changed and gays could come out in public without (with less?) harassment. A change in the law can subsequently alter most people's behaviour and a change in peoples' perceptions or behaviour can force a change in the law. If you can spot which comes first, you could be the prime mover in a brand new market!

The founder directors of Clone Zone didn't know all this stuff about changes in the law creating ideas for new businesses at the time. Neither did they know that sociological change is another opportunity source for innovative business ideas. It just so happened that they wanted to run their own show and their idea of selling things to gay men was facilitated by the existence of gay clubs that could not have legally existed a few years before. So, out with the trestle tables and off to the clubs to sell products of interest to those on the gay scene.

However, as you read through this book you will realise that you do not really need to spot the gap in the market before starting up your company. Before you learnt to drive it would have been difficult to plan the least troublesome route across town. Once you start driving you become more aware of the factors that make a route troublesome, and increasingly you spot the opportunities and the gaps that make driving across town much easier.

Beware of the obvious opportunity. If you spot an obvious gap in the market it might exist because nobody has been able to fill it, or those that have tried have failed and gone bust. Check it out by asking around.

Change is a source of new business ideas. The people who create new companies are all different, and presented with the same changes in the world in which they live, they will each perceive different opportunities. When an opportunity arises and more than one person spots it, it is likely that no two people will address it in exactly the same way. Each will format the idea to fit their capabilities and their likes and dislikes, their past experience and their future desires. The result is that businesses that are apparently the same are invariably different in some significant way.

At about the same time that the Clone Zone founders were setting up their business targeting the gay market, another company appeared on the scene. Chris Graham-Bell and Alex McKenna launched a gay magazine that grew, over the years, into a substantial publishing company and, like Clone Zone's retail company, they targeted the gay market. The same sociological and legal changes were exploited in two quite different ways by two different groups of people.

Avoid sitting around all day trying to think of a gap in the market. Try another approach by pretending you are a doctor and try to diagnose illnesses. Look for what you or others might consider symptoms of something that is wrong. Ask others for their 'bug list'. What irritates them, what do they feel could be done better? What products or services do they feel are missing from their lives? If that makes you think of a written questionnaire, please don't do it. The thought of you wasting your time with a set of preconceived questions, whilst simultaneously irritating your victims, makes me feel ill.

You will only get the really effective ideas by talking, in person, face-to-face, to other people. Having a conversation with five people is more effective than a written questionnaire sent to 500 people. Within a face-to-face conversation the amount of information that you will get from body language is vast and you won't even realise that you have got most of it. However, it feeds your intuition, giving you a feeling for the marketplace, a resource which you ignore at your peril when running a business.

If you are in the habit of reading biographies of famous entrepreneurs then you will have wondered how they succeeded when many of them are so lacking in education. Most seem to have left school early – or been kicked out – and nearly all make a point of saying that they have never read a book about business. So how did they succeed? What is the source of their knowledge and where is it located, the knowledge that they must have relied upon in order to get to the top? They practised and they learnt by making mistakes and by creating successes; they began to understand the mechanisms of business. They might not have been able to relate it verbally to others, but they got to know how things work, intuitively.

Why do people start their own companies? What drives them to take such a deliberate and demanding step, one which apparently carries with it a great deal of risk, not just financial but of the embarrassment of public failure? It seems that most men and many women would like to start their own company. But what normal, intelligent human being voluntarily gives up a well-paid job to risk all on a venture that might not work out too well? Especially when they are used to being cosseted within a large organisation, replete with support staff, well-furnished and well-equipped offices and lots of colleagues with whom to socialise, both inside and outside the workplace. Well, sometimes working in a large company is not always as comfortable as it might be.

Take the tale of the accountant who worked for a long-established construction firm that had been around for more than 100 years. The company employed all trades including bricklayers, carpenters, plumbers, electricians, plasterers, painters and decorators. Like all good accountants he decided to investigate the profit contribution from each of the trades. Having completed the project, it showed that plumbing was by far the most profitable trade for the company and could be made even more profitable as the prices being charged were much less than the market rates.

Our bean counter, naturally feeling quite proud of his work, wrote up his report and presented it to the directors of the company. He waited for the gasps of astonishment and the round of applause and back-slapping. Not a sound. Then, a bit of throat-clearing followed by outright rejection along the lines of, "We are a full-service building company and have been so for 100 years. We are not just a plumbing company – the plumbers are there to be part of the team, to support the efforts of the whole company. We do not want to create a bunch of prima donnas who look down on everybody else" The cuckoo in the nest was spotted as soon as the egg was laid and quickly ejected.

And guess what the accountant did? Predictably, he resigned a little later, having laid his plans and gathered some information. Within a month he had set up a plumbing company that grew like a eucalyptus tree. Within a few years the new company was more that half the size of the 'parent' company and making just about the same level of profits.

This is not an unusual case; employers frequently reject major ideas put forward by employees. One reason why this happens is that managers become comfortable in their present positions and change is not welcome in their comfort zone. The company may be operating to an 'industry recipe' which has become deeply embedded in the minds of managers. Change represents disturbance and the status quo is endangered. This is, of course, perfectly true; there is danger in change.

Major problems arise when the employee is more intelligent or faster-moving than the boss. After all, who wants to take orders from a dodo? The level of frustration builds up a head of steam in the employee and the safety valve is going to blow sooner or later. So the employee releases the pressure by leaving the job and setting up his own company, thereby increasing his longevity at a stroke – or should I say before the stroke. Self-imposed stress is OK, but stress imposed by others is the dangerous stuff.

A van salesman, selling into retailers, was so successful that his commission-based income exceeded the salary that his boss was paid. Instead of awarding the salesman with a gold star the boss cut his territory in two, giving half to another salesman. Just how daft can a boss get? Our van salesman resigned on the spot and got a job with a multi-national manufacturer of catering equipment. He was very successful in this job, too, but the company decided to close a depot and he was made redundant.

Our ill-treated salesman determined that he would never again work for any boss. He set up a company selling catering equipment, including some of the same product that he had been selling for the multi-national company. He was carrying the knowledge of customers and product acquired in his previous job and consequently created sales revenue immediately. He used his own small apartment as his office and rented a lock-up garage to use as his stores. A few years later he was a millionaire, with an indoor swimming pool that could comfortably hold 200 people for a private party.

Some people start up companies whilst they are working for someone else. They do their research whilst with an employer and conduct their own new business outside normal working hours. However, a one-time colleague of mine went the whole hog. His job as an employee allowed him a great deal of freedom of movement and provided he came up with the results he received his monthly salary. This guy was so competent that he built a company employing a dozen or so people whilst doing his 'full-time' job. When he was ready he left his employer to run his business full time. If they awarded the Purple Heart for balls in business he would surely have been a recipient.

Building a business satisfies the natural creative urges and many entrepreneurs use expressions to describe their motivation such as 'painting a picture' or 'producing a play – a piece of theatre'.

Good old materialism acts as a major motivator to spur you on to start your own outfit. To own that amazing automobile, the one that glides majestically, not the one that coughs, splutters and rattles when it moves. The thought of a large, pink house overlooking the Florida intra-costal inlets motivates a great many owner-managers and keeps them going through troubled times. Some even hanker after an entire sub-tropical island all to themselves. Bear in mind, though, that if you are going into business purely for the money, this desire might conflict with the patience that you will need to build a sound business. Resist the temptation to spend it before you've got it. Relying on money as the only motivator may work for you, but generally it doesn't. You may need the other motivators.

Leaving college is another life-changing event that inspires people to start up a business. Paul was an arts graduate who couldn't find a decent job after graduation. In order to provide the basics of life he took up with a friend, a poet, and together they worked as cleaners in London. The customer base was restaurants and from time to time they would be asked to perform minor maintenance jobs, which they carried out successfully. As penniless ex-students they would do anything to earn a buck.

At one point they were asked to repair a commercial dishwashing machine, even though this was a bit out of their league – an artist and a poet are not the first people that you would turn to for a plumbing and electrical repair. Instead of getting on with the repair, they would spend the day playing with the magnetic letters on the door. But the intrepid Paul decided to have a go at the dishwasher and completed a perfect repair. Ten years later he had sales revenues of millions derived from running a national team of service engineers.

Here's another, somewhat different, example. Three guys came through college together and, post PhD, two of them joined a major international consultancy firm. Their first assignment was in a large practice of architects and whilst working on this assignment they gradually absorbed the culture of the architects and began to understand their ways of working. Architects produce a huge number of images that frequently need to be recovered in order to make a PowerPoint presentation or to blow up a picture to the size of a wall, or any of a variety of different uses. Our two graduates became aware of the difficulties that the architects were experiencing in getting hold of the right image, of the right size, of the right resolution and suitable for the purpose they had in mind. They analysed and defined the problem and the solution. After their consultancy project finished they left the consultancy practice, enjoined their third partner and wrote the software for an image management system specifically for architectural practices. They had a business up and running within a year and had gained a major market share within three years.

By the way, if you are thinking that a college degree confers an advantage on you in relation to starting your own company – it doesn't. There is very little correlation between having a college education and creating a successful company.

Most entrepreneurs start their businesses based on an existing business with which they are familiar. They engage in a bit of creative copying, taking the idea and giving it a creative twist to make it different in some way. Although it is very desirable, for reasons that we shall discuss later, to have a difference built in to the business, the initial motivation of the entrepreneur in introducing a difference is more personal. They do not want others to accuse them of simply counterfeiting someone else's business ideas, hence the creative twist. There is no pride in being seen as a copycat.

When the entrepreneur uses the memory of his previous employing company, he faces a considerable difficulty which is not immediately apparent. He cannot hope to copy his previous company exactly since he does not have access to all the information. This is because he does not have access to the instructions indicating the necessary procedures to build a replica company. He only has access to the product of the instructions and can only copy what he perceives. The instructions for building the particular company are lost in the labyrinth of twists and turns made by the company as it grew. If he did have the instructions it is unlikely that he would have all the necessary resources to create an exact copy.

Humans have a need to fill gaps and where the information is not available the gaps are filled by assumptions. These assumptions become 'facts' before very long – that is, they become false memories.

In biology, there is a built-in genetic instruction that tells your left leg when to stop growing. If such an instruction were to be omitted due to faulty replication of the genes, then you might develop a 40 foot leg on one side. Although you would become famous very quickly you would not be very efficient at going about your normal business. In a real business one tiny piece of information missed, or misinterpreted, from the copy could seriously impede the new venture.

If you are intending to start a business based on what you now do as an employee, be aware that the memory you are about to carry forward will be filled with flaws, misconceptions and assumptions. It may well have already set you on tracks that you are not even aware of, such as the industry recipes and company culture that may lead you ineluctably to where you do not want to go. If you have worked for only one or two companies you will have modelled yourself on their behaviour patterns. Consequently, you will be totally unaware of the many different ways that managers in different companies behave. Company cultures can vary even more widely; what seems normal to you might appear extraordinary to someone from a different company.

There is an advantage in not being able to copy another existing company exactly. Without the assembly instructions you will introduce differences that will make your company unique and you will find your niche. The business world is never full.

Chapter 3

The Truman Show

So, what's new? Creativity is new. Innovation is new. But what's the difference? Creativity is producing something that has not been produced before, something novel. It is usually a product of two or more elements combined in a juxtaposition that has not been seen before. Such a product is always creative. Whether it is seen as creative or not is dependent on the audience, those who perceive the thing. If they have seen one before they will judge it as non-creative. If they have never seen one before and they do not understand it, nor like it, or it offends their sensibilities they may voice an opinion that it is not creative. Typically, it will be described as 'garbage'.

Innovation, on the other hand, is the creation of something that is new, useful and valued in its own time.

The trouble with creativity is that its appreciation lies entirely in the perception of the beholder. Different people will express different opinions as to its quality and hence its value. Artists have been faced with this problem since art began. In business, it is one of the primary reasons why graphic artists have such a hard time persuading their customers to pay a proper price. When faced with a panel of managers, all of whom ascribe a different value to the product, the graphic artist has to identify the decision-maker quickly and concentrate on persuading that person.

Media devices have been created to guide public taste, including newspapers, magazines and television, along with radio and discussion groups. Driving the media are the (self) appointed cultural judges, whose names are well known in the art world. Any artists trying to get their work accepted as having a value will be judged by these influencers and opinion formers, whose thumbs will either be down or up.

In business, there is also a bench of self-appointed judges who give tacit permission for products to be sold. Here is a quotation from *The Times* (London), 18/6/2005: "In Britain, Dasani bottled water was first introduced and then withdrawn, after the public discovered, via the media judges, that it came from a Sidcup tap". There are also, of course, properly appointed regulators and judges, with published regulations, laws and internationally agreed standards, that only allow products of a suitable quality to be sold.

When engaging in the act of producing innovations always bear in mind that the product you produce must be acceptable to the market in which you intend to sell it. Ideally, advertising the product should come after you have tried the influencers and opinion formers and got them on your side. The media can make or break a new product quickly, so talk to them or get your public relations person to do so on your behalf.

In general, there is very little chance of inventing a new product and turning it into a commercial success. Most new products, even those created by the largest companies in the world, fail to become commercially viable. It is better to start with an established product and to make incremental changes over time. Later on in the book, in the Reactive Phase, we will come to the ways of creating meaningful innovation.

Take the greatest care when considering new technologies as the basis for a new business. If they are likely to be popular they will attract a great many new businesses and you will end up on a bandwagon. When you rush in, attempting to be first, you may find that the new technology has lots of bugs and that it takes many years for these to be eradicated. Meanwhile, you might have run out of cash and enthusiasm.

New technologies also create conditions conducive to leap-frogging. You might base your business start-up on a particular technology and six months later more new developments make your product redundant. One minute you think you've cracked it, next minute you are out of business.

New technological knowledge is a very difficult thing to exploit and the commercial applications may take many years to manifest themselves. New knowledge also needs a market of people with a propensity to dive straight in and buy the first of the products. These people are known collectively as 'early adopters' and you need to know how to get to them first.

You have to identify the need, or desire, for the new technology before you start to build a company based on it. It may just be a fad or a slightly longer lasting fashion. It is very expensive to try and educate the market and, as a start up company, it is highly unlikely that you would have the resources to engage in such a strategy. Whilst you are educating the market, someone else might develop a simpler version, with less features, and you get leap-frogged.

Most people have had different experiences in their lives, have different belief systems, different interests and so on. We are all pretty well unique, in practice. The following narrative illustrates this human feature. Ted was a wine buyer and his job required him to travel in Italy, seeking out new and interesting wines. His wife owned a fashion shoe shop in the UK and she sometimes travelled with him for the purpose of buying Italian fashion shoes. Whilst on one of these trips they noticed that Benetton stores were operating in most Italian towns. Ted and his wife had the confidence and business acumen to approach Benetton and offer to run some Benetton franchises in the UK. Benetton agreed and Ted and his wife were the first to introduce Benetton into the UK, subsequently making a great success of the venture.

We all have some unique combination of situation or experience that will lead to genuine innovations. Introducing foreign products or stores to your home country or taking a home-based product abroad can be effective cross-cultural innovations. The wok, originating from China, is another example of a cross-cultural transfer. These products have already proved their acceptability within one culture. The only risk left for you is the possibility that they might not be acceptable in your chosen geographic area. Something that is acceptable in New York City may not be appreciated to the same extent in Bryson City.

Opportunities can arise frequently in more established product market sectors. Most established sectors operate to recipes that are standardised across many companies. The place to look is not so much at the products but the processes, being aware that anybody within the sector who comes up with a new idea will probably be rejected. The existing companies have invested too much in their processes to abandon them now. But if you can find a process improvement and start your own business based on that, then you stand a good chance of success. It might be as simple as a better form of packaging or a different approach to delivery.

There is an accepted recipe in the world of innovation itself. It says that in order to create something new the inventor must have spent at least ten years working on it. There is another way of looking at this often repeated recipe. After ten years work, the industry judges accept the innovator as an expert, one who has acquired the credibility for his ideas to be adopted. However, the innovation might well have taken place well before the ten years rite of passage. After all, who would accept a new idea from someone still wet behind the years?

Beware of falling into the trap of thinking that because some novel inventions have resulted in very rich inventors, that all new inventions will produce the same result. We all have a tendency to use hindsight selectively, and whilst we remember the winners, we erase the huge number of losers from history, as if they never existed.

Demographic analysis is a very seductive technique in market research. It is concerned with the characteristics of a population, including age, sex, occupation, location and so on. Demographic forecasting, showing trends in the characteristics of a population, is relatively easy, which is why it is so attractive. Marketing managers everywhere are furiously looking in their little red books and making revealing demographic forecasts and deducing remarkable good product market strategies for use when the time comes. You can easily forecast the size of the working-age population in twenty years time (they are all already born), and if it is greater than it is now you will probably deduce that there will be more wealth created at that time in the future. Isn't that wonderful? We can now forecast that our sales revenue will be 60% greater in real terms in twenty years time. We have been growing wealthier year after year, at the rate of two or three percent per annum, for several hundred years. This working age cohort is very important, we are told by the forecasters, as over the last few decades they have been forecasting all sorts of amazing things. Somehow these nuggets of useful information have passed me by. They also seem to have by-passed the hundreds of companies with which I have worked.

Create your ideas for today, not for the future. Trying to take advantage of future demographics and creating a product for a market in five years time is futile. The future will not be as you think it will be, regardless of definite forecasts of the age cohorts at specific times. Age is pretty meaningless, it's behaviour that matters. When I was a kid a man of 50 was considered old and would have retired from all active pursuits, and that is what the forecasters would have projected. However, medical advances, changing social attitudes and greater wealth allows men of 60 and older to take up water skiing for the first time and behave in entirely different ways from that which would have been predicted.

All the many books written about creativity proclaim that innovation is a good thing. But it is only a good thing if it performs well and you cannot know that until after the event. The examples in the books on creativity are examples of successful innovation such as Steve Jobs at Apple, Edwin Land inventing the Polaroid camera and, most frequently, those darned yellow half-sticky things invented by 3M. The same examples keep surfacing, indicating that there is a shortage of such events. Having listened to entrepreneurs, over and over again, describe their lucky breaks as a result of their cleverness and hard work I am very suspicious of *post hoc* rationalisations. You have to be there and almost inside their heads to know how it really happened. Where are all the books that concern themselves with the failures? Who are all the people who spent ten or twenty years of their lives developing an innovation and created an effect equal to zero?

Most of the oft-quoted innovations, such as those above, just suddenly fell out of the sky. All are inventions and ideas that had little or no history. There are thousands of such inventive ideas constantly arising, the vast majority of which never result in even the smallest amount of development. Most just stay in the head of the inventor, some might make it onto paper, with some sketches being produced. Some might even commence development, but virtually none ever reach the marketplace. The majority of new products are incremental developments of existing products and nearly all are produced by technical research in the research and development laboratories of large companies. Small, start-up companies with new inventions do not seem to get off the ground. Taking an existing idea and tweaking it is a more successful technique and a much easier route to a successful business.

Start-up businesses often start with a very mundane idea. Whilst natural things can only evolve naturally, business can be encouraged to do so purposefully. The evolution comes about by allowing the close external environment to affect beliefs, thoughts and actions. You have built your own world from all that you know and from all that you have experienced, directly or vicariously, and this world is not the same as the worlds that other people inhabit.

In Peter Weir's film *The Truman Show*, Jim Carrey plays the part of Truman Burbank, who has been born into a reality soap opera. Truman does not know that he is the star of the soap and that the cameras are on him 24/7. Neither does he know that all the people that he interacts with on a daily basis are professional actors. When Christophe, the director of the soap opera, is asked, "Why do you think Truman has never come close to discovering the true nature of his world... ?" Christophe replies, "We accept the reality of the world with which we are presented. It's as simple as that"

There is a boundary to Truman's world, but he does not perceive it. When Truman looks around him he sees reality, whilst we, being outside his world, know that he is looking at scenery. However, as Christophe says to Truman, "There is no more truth out there then there is in the world I created for you" No more truth, maybe, but it is a different truth.

We can become aware of others' worlds only by moving the scenery of our own, and to create a business which serves the customer we must perceive their scenery, the content of their world. Since we are the actors in our make-believe world, we must engage other people in order to move the scenery. We need a crew of stage-hands and you know what they do: they 'break the set' so the show can move on. In your case, they break your mind-set.

Most businesses take their mundane idea and allow other people to interact with the idea and develop it to suit those other people – potential customers. The mundane idea is the business world that you inhabit and the other people that you interact with are the stage-hands that help you move the scenery. So recruit some 'stage-hands' to test your view of the world and see how they can persuade you to change it for the better. As we go about our lives we base all our activities on assumptions and we have a tendency to ignore evidence that conflicts with those assumptions. This is the essential reason why you should consult with and test your ideas against other people.

The stage-hands should be as different, one from the other, as you can possibly find, ranging across age, sex, occupation, nationality, pastimes and any other differences. If you have an idea of who your customers are going to be then make sure that you include some of these types. Customers are people and people like people who are like them, so you will have to change to be like them, not the other way round. Educating your customers can be a futile and very expensive pursuit; you must let them educate you.

The stage hands must be the sort of people who are willing to engage with you in a benevolent, yet critical, manner and you may need to devise some rewards or incentives to encourage their participation. Encourage them to challenge your thinking and your ideas. You do not have to adapt your ideas or your behaviour to everything that everybody says to you, but you must consider it.

Present your ideas to them and ask for their comments. If they are hesitant or reluctant, then press them, remembering that negative comments are frequently more meaningful than positive comments. Try to sell your idea to the customer types and if they agree to buy, find out why. Likewise, if they do not buy, ask them to tell why they didn't. Ask them what you would have to offer in order for them to happy about buying from you.

A group of stage-hands should be with you throughout all the phases of growth, changing the scenery as appropriate, and the composition of the group will change to meet the changing worlds that the business must operate within. In this, the Creative Phase, spread your net wide in recruiting stage-hands; don't stick to the same people all the time. Bear in mind that the external world is always changing and your internal world, your perceived reality, may get out of kilter with the worlds of others. We have to make assumptions in order to make decisions, but assumptions made for one decision may still be in use, inappropriately, long after they should have been dumped.

Daniel Isenberg, writing in the *Harvard Business Review*, says that bosses, in order to help their decision-making, "develop and maintain an extensive interpersonal network". You will notice that, in many of the examples that I mention in this book, the original product or service is modified later at the suggestion of some person other than the entrepreneur.

Resist the temptation, if it is one, to engage in brainstorming sessions with your stage-hands. Just listen to their views and then do your thinking on your own. In that way you will be able to arrive at ideas and make decisions that fit you and your customers exactly. If you allow others to make decisions for you, you will find that the implementation of those decisions will never feel quite right. You know the experience of thinking, 'that doesn't feel quite right'? Well, if you feel like that you are dead right, so go with the feeling.

Innovation runs through a growing company from birth and is the essence of life to the enterprise. In the Reactive Phase we again address innovation, in the appropriate way for that phase. At the end of the Processes Phase we again address incremental innovation, and in the last section of this book, the Divisions Phase, we return to the creation of new businesses in considerable detail.

But do not jump forward to these sections. Start to learn the patience, and persistence, that you will need for survival right now and work your way through all the phases in the order in which they have been set out. Then you can go back to the beginning of the book, read it through again and you will realise that Phases of Growth are different from stages of growth. Phases stay with you and you will need to adopt the different behaviours of each phase as required, over and over again, as your company continues to grow.

Chapter 4

Why People Buy Stuff

Why do people buy stuff? If you start up a business and you don't really know why people buy stuff, your offer might consist of things that nobody wants to buy. Imagine if you open your shop doors onto the mall and nobody at all comes through the door. It's a nightmare thought.

Most people who start up new companies try to offer something that they think people will want to buy. But some people don't try and work out what sort of things people want to buy, and they are called 'inventors'. If you ask people what they want to buy they will usually indicate that they are already satisfied in all respects. If you press them, they will offer flippant and maybe downright silly suggestions. Others may be more earnest and rack their brains for something that they think you might want to hear. Many a posh chocolate shop has been opened based on the results of 'market research' in the mall or on the street. "Oh, what a lovely idea!" they exclaim, "a chocolate shop on our street. Of course we will come and buy your beautiful chocolates". No, they do not. They continue to buy their chocolates from the supermarket and they feel very happy at having pleased you by telling you what you wanted to hear.

Another approach, one that seems to elude most peoples' minds, is to create an offer that will help people avoid something. Consider why men and women buy razors and after-shave lotions. Not because they want to buy them, but because, respectively, they do not want hairy faces or hairy legs. They will express their want as a negative, although what they really, really want is to be more beautiful and attractive in order to achieve sexual, social or business success.

All you have to do is ask people to write down all the things that bug them now. Suggest to them that you will contact them in a month's time to ask them to do the same exercise again. Some will keep notes, their personal bug list, during that time and it will be a considered list. You can select a wide range of people of all ages, income brackets, nationalities, occupations and so on. But if you want your customers to be of a particular type, then you can select only that type.

Instead of designing a product or service offer and then trying to find a market to sell it to, you can approach it from a different angle. You can decide who will be your customers, a type that you will feel comfortable dealing with and they will be the very people that you will find selling to very easy. When they provide their bug lists, they are describing their needs in a negative form, like "I hate hairy legs!"

Now all you have to do is to ask them what their ideal solutions would be to rid themselves of the bugs and they will give you a fairly realistic description of the product or service that you could sell to them. The rest is up to you; the customers have given you directions to Shangri-la, the ultimate goal of the entrepreneur, one that confers long life.

There are lots of things that people do not want, including pain. The relief of pain is big business, as demonstrated by the giant pharmaceutical companies that dominate the stock markets of the world. The relief of pain is small business, as practised by the acupuncturist or chiropractor, working from that little room under the hairdressers. The relief of pain can also be medium sized business, with the chain of pharmacies fronting the many treatment rooms within which are the manipulators and chiropractors and psychotherapists.

Home deliveries relieve the burden of the customer and are an essential service to allow sales by mail, telephone or the internet, by which means the customers avoid the pain of shopping in the cold and rain. Can you deliver something that is not usually delivered, thereby relieving the pains of your customers?

From a positive perspective, what do people need? Our needs are ultimately driven by our genetic programming, modified by hormonal effects within the womb. Our wants and desires originate from the same sources and are further modified by our early environment. The word 'ultimate' is important here; it means that we are dealing with the most basic cause of buying stuff.

Humans are conceived with a genetic imperative to survive and to procreate. In order to obey this imperative we must, in approximate order of importance, obtain liquids, food and procreative sex. To enhance our survival chances we need to provide ourselves and our families with shelter from adverse climates and protection from predators.

To enhance our ability to sexually procreate we need a social life – we must meet with the opposite sex. The most attractive people find it easier to procreate, giving rise to a desire in most people to be better than their sexual rivals. Being 'better than' means leading others in some way, like having smoother legs if you are a woman. Since this is book is primarily about business, not genetics and psychology, let us agree to allow a little digression, back to the future.

The desire of people to make money is one of the motivating factors for starting up in business and selling stuff to others. Those who do not want to start a business sell themselves for money – they get a job. Banks and other financial institutions compete for the pleasure of looking after peoples' money, for a small fee, thereby satisfying the desire for security. Could your business make, or save, your customers' money? Could it provide extra security for other peoples' money? From personal financial advisors to giant banks, from stockbrokers to stock exchanges, they all charge transaction fees for moving other peoples' money about.

Making money is only one side of the coin; the other side is saving money. If your business intends to sell to other businesses (B2B) then saving your customer money is almost a prerequisite of completing the sale. What you sell to them may not be the cheapest, but when they buy it must reduce their costs overall. If you are selling to small businesses they may not be able to evaluate the savings that they will make and it will be down to you to provide the evidence. This becomes part of your sales pitch.

A general form of behaviour that drives the commercial world is the constant desire for variety. Why do we need so many different types of restaurant? Why do they all have to have a fairly extensive menu? Why do we get fed up, metaphorically speaking, when we have tried everything on the menu? Restaurant owners describe this as 'menu fatigue' and therefore good chefs change their menus frequently.

Have you ever noticed that, having eaten a substantial main course for dinner, you refuse second helpings? You protest that you couldn't eat another thing and that is exactly how you feel. However, when three different desserts appear on the table you begin to salivate and pronounce that you will only have a little bit of that one. If you are a normal human being you will succumb to all three and still find space for chocolates and coffee. A natural survival driver pushes you to eat variety whenever you get the chance and it over-rules your fullness neurotransmitters when different foods are offered.

It all makes sense when you consider the ultimate cause of our eating behaviours. We must eat to survive and if we eat only one type of food we will surely miss out on many of the vitamins and minerals that support life. If we don't have enough sodium in our bodies we will die. If we never consume vitamin C, then we will get scurvy, our teeth will fall out and we will probably starve to death as a result.

Restaurant advisers, usually celebrity chefs, will often advise inexperienced restaurant owners to cut back their menus from forty dishes to ten. In that way they will reduce their costs substantially. So they take the advice, their costs drop and their profits rise. Wonderful! But after the celebrity chef has disappeared over the horizon in a cloud of dust and small pebbles, profits start to fall gradually. Regular diners are leaving longer gaps between attendances and new people only visit two or three times and are never seen again. The competition is offering more variety (or is perceived to be doing so).

The search for variety in sexual partners translates into all sorts of mechanisms that are provided in the form of businesses. All living things, from animals to humans, survive best by having a variety of genes. This means that if a family has a varied selection of genes originating from different fathers or mothers it is unlikely that one type of disease will wipe out all of them. Different genetic make-up helps some to avoid the disease. The entire fashion industry, including jewellery and cosmetics, is fuelled by this ultimate driver of sexual variety. Fast car companies and the popular music scenes are commercial expressions of the exploitation of this ultimate driver.

If you understand the ultimate causes you can build your business promotions around those causes. Determine what ultimate drivers are motivating your customers to engage with your business and go there to get ideas for satisfying your customer.

Humans are omnivores, in that they can eat almost anything that grows and, consequently, they are hunter gatherers. However, we differ from other animals in several respects, one of which is our ability to imitate each other in virtually all activities. Once upon a time a human discovered how to create fire probably, like many great discoveries, by accident. Another human, nearby, observes the fire maker and imitates the process; by trial and error they might even improve the efficiency of the process.

Good ideas get passed to others and adopted, whilst poor ideas disappear. The ability to copy ideas from others confers an advantage to humans in respect of survival and reproduction. If you are the only guy in the village who can create fire and it happens to be wintertime, then you will probably not die of the cold, but others might. You will also have a head-start in acquiring mates, who will have a burning desire to be near you.

Copycats rule OK. Notice how, even today, the copycats are held in the highest esteem because they are the best at copying other people. We call them film stars.

If you tell your potential customer that the luggage that you make is the best in the world, they will think, "Well, she would say that, wouldn't she?", not really being convinced. However, if a photograph appears in the magazines showing a top film actress leaving Charles de Gaulle airport, in Paris and she is wheeling your luggage, then you will probably make a sale. You have exploited 'referent power' to convince your customer, assuming that she wants to copy that particular film actress. Even if she thinks little of the particular actress, the customer can rationalise: "If it's good enough for her, it's good enough for me"

The use of referent power exploits the customers' desire to copy people who appear to be more important, more desirable or more fashionable. Or better in any way that the customer values. You can reach the tipping point of sales, the point when suddenly everybody must have one of the things that you are selling, by carefully planned use of referent power. The desire to imitate is very, very strong and not just amongst the young. Perfectly sensible older people will habitually frequent certain restaurants and ski resorts because someone they would like to be associated with already goes there. So, send your products to famous people – free of charge. They might be seen using them or wearing them.

The desire for status – leadership – comes in the material forms of a big house, big car, big bank balance and famous friends. But, if your business is tuition, you can sell a better university degree on the same basis.

The closer you get to the actual behaviour of buying, the more proximate are the causes. For instance, people want to save time and they want to be clean and a shower, rather than a bath, satisfies both desires. They want to be safe, so they stay in a house with a burglar alarm and locks on the windows. They want to be amused, which desire can be satisfied by a 40" TV screen, fed from their own computer containing their music, video and family photo collections.

Most people will do their best to avoid pain or discomfort, loss of money and loss of their reputations. They will pay good money to avoid these, but I am not suggesting that you consider the 'loss of reputation' option as an exhortation to set up a blackmail business.

The next stage in explaining why people buy stuff brings us into the realm of marketing. Since this is not a book on marketing, we cannot go too deeply into that subject, so here's just a bit.

Somebody who needs to satisfy their thirst might bypass the water tap and spend their money on a Coca-Cola. Why? Maybe it's perceived as 'cool' and is a badge of group membership. They might be ostracised by their friends if they drink something else.

The reason might be more prosaic. Coca-Cola is the only drink available in the vending machine. Point-of-sale is the place where people make their buying decisions when it is a simple purchase. Impulse buys in supermarkets are encouraged by packaging and shelf position and proximity to essentials.

You may have noticed that I have not addressed the reasons why businesses buy stuff. That is because, firstly, businesses do not buy stuff. But the people that work in businesses do buy stuff and they are subject to the same motivations as when they are consumers. However, they are different because the constraints of the business processes and culture and the fact that they are not spending their own money play a major part in their decision making. In the Reactive Phase the reasons why businesses buy stuff is discussed in some detail. In the Processes Phase we will address the mechanism for reducing irrational behaviour in a business.

Section 2

Analysis Phase

Chapter 5

Of Mice and Men

You will, no doubt, have heard about the 'vision' that all successful entrepreneurs must have in order to succeed in business. It is a curiosity that, when seeking examples of entrepreneurs who succeeded because of having created a company vision, I could not find one. However, I did find one extremely successful company that had been going for over 20 years and they were only starting to write their vision statement. Simultaneously, they were talking to two prospective buyers of the company, the directors having decided to retire early, provided they could get a good enough price.

It is also curious that the hundreds of entrepreneurs that I know pretty well seem to have all overlooked the creation of a vision, that apparently basic requirement for success. Yet these people are as rational in their behaviour as could be expected, in the context of their environment and their capabilities. They are all aware of the concept of the company vision and they just ignore it. Why do they all avoid creating a vision for their companies?

When you think of the phrase 'a vision' you probably think of paranormal phenomena, in particular in the context of religion. The principle behind a shared vision is the principle that underlies the structure of a religious organisation. Once the common vision of the desirable objective is installed in the individual, each person will be able to act in concert with their fellows without further reference to an authority figure. The vision becomes part of their belief system, in the same way that we believe the sun will rise each day and, consequently, plan our behaviour according to that belief. It is not necessary that a superior authority to direct us in our actions. In humans, the combination of beliefs and desires produces intentions to behave in ways that are compatible with their beliefs and desires.

Once a vision is internalised within the person, it is generally fixed for a considerable time. Visions do not change in response to the changing environment, provided that the group structures remain in place. Group structures are maintained by a common culture, reinforced by legends, myths, symbols and rituals. They do not change when the world around them changes and they attempt to impose themselves on the world.

This creates a serious problem for the growing company, which must be light on its feet and very responsive to the world in which it operates. Change, both internal and external, becomes difficult once the vision of the future is installed. External change is resisted and the possibility of internal change is not even considered. If a company making gas lamps for domestic users had a vision which proclaimed that "There will be a Wilberforce gas lamp in every home" it would have certainly failed by now.

Where did all this stuff about company visions come from, if they are counter-productive in practice? People seek causes – for everything. When an analyst turns his beady eye on a successful entrepreneur, one who has founded a successful company, he encounters a problem. He cannot work out how it was done. How did this character create such an enormously successful corporation? The analyst has to write in his report that he could not figure out how it was done; maybe it was just luck. Have you ever read a report which said, after the headings, 'This report is necessarily short because, having studied the problem, I find myself completely baffled. End of report. You will probably agree that this is the most unlikely outcome of the analysis and probably results in the analyst remaining unpaid.

People need causes and they constantly seek to find them. The analyst rationalises that if the structure of the organisation is this big and this complex, it cannot have been created by luck. It must have been planned. So where is the plan? The entrepreneur says there *is* no plan and there *was* no plan. The suggestion is then put to the entrepreneur that, when he started the company, he undoubtedly had a grand vision of the future in place of a plan. "I've got it, Peter!" said the analyst, "you had a grand vision of 'a book in every home' and you made it all come true" Peter sat back in his chair, smiled and said, "That is exactly how I did it. You may publish that well-known fact" The analyst sighs in relief and satisfaction – he has found his cause and it's believable, and nobody can deny it now it's been confirmed by the entrepreneur.

When you have worked closely with many entrepreneurs you will find that the mask of omnipotence slips, especially when placing oneself on the outside of a bottle of good wine. Then, it is quietly admitted that, "I have been very, very lucky in business" They know they never planned it, yet here they are at the top of the hill, unaware of how it really happened. When you have read this book you will know how it happens.

The power of the future vision is supposed to provide the creative tension that creates the motivation, the drive that makes everyone work in unison towards the same end. Yet there is little emotional motivation in a long distance goal. Long distance motivation is purely cerebral and most people do not respond to it. The striving to be the best, the pursuit of perfection observed in champions, is more likely a product of exposure to a lot of intra-uterine testosterone rather than to a grand vision of the future. The envisioning used by a tennis player who is serving is short, sharp and now.

A vision of the desired future is, by its nature, long-term in relation to the rewards of achievement. That means there is a huge expenditure of time, energy, money and other resources now in order to benefit from a future reward. In essence, a vision is a form of deferred gratification, and deferred gratification does not come naturally to human beings.

The desire to take the rewards now is a very old bit of genetic coding, operating through the limbic system, part of our brain that deals with emotions. In primitive times eating the food now made sense, since it might not be there tomorrow (Walmart and Tesco didn't operate in those days). Deferring gratification is a cerebral operation, requiring rational activity in the prefrontal cortex of the brain. That's why really clever people put money into their pension funds and less clever people postpone or ignore that form of investment. However, if the world became a really dangerous place and there was a strong chance that we might not survive for long, it would be better to rely on our limbic system and seize the day. Growing a company is a bit like living in the Neolithic past in that you never know what's over the next ridge, so you have to react quickly to events.

The observed reality of the formation of a common vision of the future, with the concurrent indoctrination of the ideas, is that it will lead to 'groupthink'. These ideas will survive without challenge, the world will change and the company will be left behind, a bereft brontosaurus bellowing mournfully across the primeval swamp.

In 1776, during the American War of Independence, General Burgoyne led a British army south from Canada, his intention being to capture the city of Albany, which lies on the Hudson River. He had a detailed plan laid out, including sailing his fleet of ships down Lake Champlain to within 100 miles of Albany. He had worked out a clever tactic to take Fort Ticonderoga, which was successful. He and his army then set off to march to Albany. However, the going was very tough; the terrain was very difficult, with swamps, streams, rivers, dense woods and undergrowth hindering their passage. Maintaining supplies was a nightmare and typically they progressed at about one mile per day. Half the men were suffering from dysentery and all were exhausted. Although Burgoyne had known that this march might be tough, it was far worse than he had planned.

On the side of the Americans things were very different. The militia was made up of local farmers, none of whom had any military training. They were armed with muskets and anything else that they could find. They had no pre-prepared plan or strategy, just an idea and desire for independence from King George III. So they just waited for Burgoyne's army. When the demoralised British reached the open spaces the militia attacked and routed the army, killing many and making prisoners of the rest.

There was a bonus for the Americans. The French were so impressed by the victory that they accepted Benjamin Franklin's proposal of a treaty. Ultimately, this led to the British General Cornwallis being defeated at Yorktown by a force made up of the armies of Washington and Lafayette, with the French fleet blockading the British ships off the coast. This was the defining moment of America's struggle for Independence, which was agreed by the British shortly afterwards.

So, a carefully thought-out plan by an experienced general, with a powerful army, was defeated by a competitor who had less in the way of resources and capabilities. The failure of the British plan was the tipping point in the War of Independence.

If you have been to university you will have learned how to write an essay, with a clear objective, and how to structure a logical argument that leads to a logical conclusion. The source material that you can use to structure your argument is fairly well defined; it is the course material that you are advised to read by your tutors. This creates an artificial world of information, finite and closed, with limited variables. In some cases, you will be advised by your tutors that if you want to achieve top marks, you will not use sources outside of the set books.

This is exactly how business plans are composed. The composer limits the variables quite arbitrarily and excludes all that he doesn't know or that he does not have time to research. The size and depth of the plan is limited by the time available to the composer, by the availability of information and the physical size and weight of the written plan document. He knows that he is excluding information that he knows. But he does not know that he is excluding information that he does not know.

Compared to being successful at gaining your university degree, the creation of your business plan goes something like this. First, you have to decide on your own subject, but how will you know that it is the right subject? Secondly, you must decide on your own objectives, but how will you know that the objectives that you choose are the right ones? How will you know if they are achievable? Thirdly, you will need to structure a logical argument or plan that will enable you to reach your objectives. You will derive your argument from the material available to you, but how will you define the 'course' materials? How widely will you range? How will you know when you have got all the relevant material?

The fact is that there are so many variables that can, and will, impinge upon your growing business that there is no way whatsoever that you can determine what they will be in advance.

You might have come across the phrase "You can never step in the same river twice" This phrase originates with Heraklitos, a Greek pre-Socratic philosopher – a more accurate translation of what he actually said is: "On stepping into rivers staying the same, other waters flow" To paraphrase, Heraclitus is saying that, whilst the rivers stay the same, the waters are always changing.

Heraklitos did not go far enough. Reality is that the rivers themselves are always changing due to erosion, but they are changing at a slower pace than the waters. However, due to a landslide, a falling boulder, an earthquake, a glacier or another reason, a river may suddenly change course or it might fork and form two rivers. Human intervention changes rivers by building dams and engaging in upstream extraction of water.

In the real world of growing companies everything is changing all the time, but some things change more slowly than others. This is what makes business so eternally fascinating. It's not love that makes the world go round; it's the Doctrine of Flux, originating from the ideas of Heraklitos, the original Dr. Flux.

The person who said that there is no more space for new companies to succeed in the world of business should be reminded of some of the things that can change. Products and services are changing, developing or disappearing all the time. Sociological propensities are continuously changing as society develops different beliefs and behaviours and exploits new products and services. Health, wealth, longevity and even the climate is changing. Politics and economics are always in a state of flux and changes are exacerbated with every change of government. All these factors, and many others, are inter-related in a web that is impossible to unravel or decipher accurately.

We all do our best to pretend that we are rational human beings and that all our decisions are the result of rational thought processes. But the truth is well known – our rationality is bounded. The world is too complicated for us to fully understand, because the processing capacity of our brains is limited; we do not have access to infinite intelligence. On a practical level, how long should we take to decide on something? We cannot take forever, so the time available is also a boundary enclosing our rationality.

Forecasts of the future are almost invariably based on information from the past. Forecasters observe something that is happening at the time of planning and extrapolate into the future. If the world is going to be the same as now, just merely extrapolated into the future, why bother to forecast? And if the world is not going to be the same in the future, then the forecast will certainly be wrong. Having inspected hundreds of business plans, I find it very interesting that all the trends included in the rationalisation are always favourable to the planners. Trends going the other way are either ignored or forecast to change to a favourable state at exactly the right time to ensure dramatic success.

Business plans can seriously limit your options. An example is a company that I observed over several years, during which it turned down or ignored some startlingly good options. The offer by a major brand to co-brand on a range of products was turned down because it was not in the business plan. An offer from a Spanish importer, which would have increased sales revenues by 20% or more, was ignored because it was not in the plan. Other opportunities were also dismissed and the business plan was pursued doggedly. The plan included a strategy based on the 80/20 rule, which states that 20% of your customers yield 80% of your profits. The business plan proposed to get rid of all the small, expensive to run customers, concentrating only on the big ones. Guess what? They got rid of the little ones and then two of the large ones decided to buy elsewhere. Yes, the company did go bust.

Why do so many people advocate the production of detailed business plans for start up businesses when there is no evidence that they contribute anything beneficial to the company? And why do some people (very few) prepare business plans for use in their business?

The answer to the first question in respect of advocating the production of a business plan is the same as the analyst and the vision. Some people, who have never run a successful business, cannot conceive of another option.

The answer to the second question is that a business plan can serve an emotional need in the entrepreneur, providing a sort of security blanket. Making all the decisions for the future, well in advance, whilst sitting in an armchair means that you don't have to make them again! That's comforting. Unfortunately, it also closes down all alternative courses of action, especially if the plan is published to staff or lenders or investors.

If you place your faith in a plan for the future then the security blanket makes you feel safe. The offset hypotheses – wearing seat belts makes drivers take careless risks – will encourage more risk-taking behaviour because you feel safer, and that can be dangerous.

In practice, most business plans are just hyperbole used to extract investment in the form of loans from banks or equity investment from business angels. There is only one sure thing about a business plan and that is that the projections of sales revenues and profits will definitely be wrong. Any thinking investor or lender will back the person, not the plan.

Some people say that preparing a business plan provides an education about the arena that you are about to enter. You might still need that information, but putting it in a plan interprets the information as static. Read the plan a few months later and it still contains the same information. It was out of date the day after you wrote it down.

Others put forward the theory that talking to experts in the field, a practice known as the 'Delphic Oracle', may give you some knowledge of the future. No, it doesn't. It has been tried by many companies and a group of 'experts' will be no more accurate in forecasting the future than any group of sensible people. The stage-hands that you have gathered around you are not there to provide you with *the* truth; they exist to provide you with alternative truths to your own beliefs. They are there just so you don't get stuck into a single-minded lemming-like rush over a cliff. Although they may have useful current information on the state of play, they will not know the future.

Adherents of the planning game advocate that in order to get to your destination you must first know where you are, where you are going to and have plotted the route that you plan to follow. The analogy of a voyage on a ship is commonly used.

On 10th April 1912 the RMS *Titanic* set sail from Southampton on her maiden voyage to New York. At 11:40 p.m. on 14th April 1912 she struck an iceberg off Newfoundland, Canada. Less than three hours later, the *Titanic* sunk to the bottom of the sea, taking 1,500 people with her.

You know where you want to go; just point the ship and go. But remember to watch out for changes in the wind and sea conditions. Look out for other ships that impede your passage or run you down, and look out for unexpected icebergs and monsters. The *Titanic* should have learned the processes necessary for crossing the Atlantic before it took on passengers. Most importantly, do not invest 1,500 passengers in something that you are doing for the first time. Or even $1500.

Answer me truthfully: do you really believe that you can accurately forecast your prices and your costs for three years ahead? Can you also forecast who your competitors will be, their exact prices over that timescale and their reaction to your presence in the market? Get real.

Goals should be yours alone; if you spread it about it restricts your decision-making options. You must retain the freedom to change the destination, as well as your course, whenever you feel the need, and if your stakeholders know that you are chopping and changing you will lose credibility in their eyes. Communicate only short-term objectives to others. The principle of deferred gratification means that emotional motivation is for now and that is more powerful than the intellectual motivation needed for a distant objective.

Ignore the visionary leader stuff. It is not the capabilities of such leaders that allow them to be inspirational leaders. They are made by their followers, the particular time and place that they inhabit and the opportunities that are available to them. When circumstances change, the visionary leader topples from his pedestal into the sands, and on the pedestal these words appear: "My name is Ozymandias, King of Kings: look on my works, ye mighty, and despair! Nothing beside remains..."

Hear what Daniel Isenberg, a senior lecturer at Harvard Business School, has to say in *The Harvard Review*, after he studied the way senior managers really think: "...managers frequently by-pass rigorous analytical planning altogether, particularly when they face difficult, novel or extremely entangled problems. When they do use analysis for a prolonged time, it is always in conjunction with intuition" I might dare to suggest that the purpose of the prolonged analysis is to provide a *post hoc* rationalisation for a decision already made. After all, these were professional, successful managers; they had to cover their asses in order to keep their jobs:.

The best laid plans of mice and men
Oft gang awry
And leave us nothing but grief and pain
For promised joy

Robert Burns, 1785

Robert Burns knew it over two hundred years ago. Why do we forget it?

Chapter 6

Searching...

There are three essential resources that you will need in order to perform any task; you will certainly need them to grow a successful company. Since these resources are generic you may have come across them elsewhere, in a different context. You will need time, you will need energy and, most importantly, you will need information. Not just data, but real, usable information, the sort that you can apply immediately and that which results in some degree of success.

Time, energy and information operate in combination with each other, with more of one allowing for less of the others. Many companies are started up by people who have very little information in respect of running a business. This does not preclude success, but it does mean that there is more reliance on the other two types of resource. It is very noticeable that these people work extremely long hours and expend a great deal of energy. They physically rush about a lot, trying to engage in several conversations with different people at the same time. They seldom take time off from work and their working days are long. An absence of holidays and a blending of the weekends into the working week is a common scenario.

The company that is started with the owner manager having little information on running a business takes a long time to grow to a self-sustaining level. Typically, such businesses take six years or more – usually more – to grow to a size that produces an appropriate income for the owner. Some haven't quite made it even after 20 years. Many fail completely before the self-sustaining stage has been reached.

In starting a company, having limited information, it would be wise to look after your energy levels by taking care of your mind and body. Try to save time by reducing your commitments to areas of your life that do not assist in the growth of your company. The more real information you can get, the less time it will take you to build your company. However, you will have to expend time and energy initially to get the information. You can short-cut the process by taking on a partner who will also gather information and share it with you. Companies that have more than one owner manager tend to grow faster than companies that have a sole founder manager.

A company that I worked with operated in the field of marketing IT and was formed by four founder directors. All the directors were highly qualified academically and capable of absorbing large amounts of complex information very quickly. They also had complementary skills. For instance, the software architect director traded information with the sales director, whose experience was gained as sales director of a multinational. Another director was a highly competent administrator. Their stated aim, from the beginning, was to grow the company for four years and then sell out. This is exactly what they achieved, each of the four directors achieving millionaire status in the process.

When you discuss your proposal for your start up company with bank managers and most business advisers you will be quizzed on the nature and extent of your market research. When you admit that you have done absolutely nothing in that respect, the bank manager will insist, and the business adviser will suggest strongly, that you choose your market and then research it to determine its size and type.

They will ask if you have done any secondary research, by which they mean 'have you been to the library and read the published market reports that are freely available'. Secondary research is desk-based research and involves reading up on the already-published stuff. This will include hard copy market studies produced by commercial research companies. Generally, secondary research is cheap research and, like most things you buy, you get what you pay for. It is frequently out of date, because it takes time to collect, analyse, publish and distribute. It is also unfocused, in respect of your proposed start up company. These reports have to cover a large area, usually national, since the publishers need to sell many copies to cover their costs and make a profit. If you are planning to operate in a smaller region or a city then they may lead you to believe things that will not be relevant to your business. The reports that you will find in the public library are probably at least a year old and are dangerous in that they may mislead rather than guide you. Be constantly aware that because information is in print it does not necessarily have the qualities of accuracy, reality or timeliness.

My apologies for returning to the subject of demographic analysis, but it is such a common trap for people creating a new company, that I feel I must emphasise it. Well-meaning advisors may also suggest that you study the demographics of the geographic area in which you plan to operate your business. This will give you information down to the level managed by your local authority. They will tell you how many people are resident in the area, their sex and age, their employment status and maybe incidence of car ownership and so on. Quoting all this hard-core information in your analysis will no doubt impress the bank manager. At least it gives him a rationale for when you default on the bank loan and he needs to justify, to his boss, the decision to make the loan.

I have just bought a book on starting up a business and it recommends that a good place to get a business idea is from the projection of demographics into the future. Specifically, it mentions that in the predictable future there will be many more people between 60 and 80 years old. It states that these people will be healthier and wealthier then the comparable age group at the current time. It concludes that you could design a product for that future time. Not on that information, you can't!

The apparent logic of demographics is seductive, but the primary thinking is wrong. The objective of market research of any sort is to forecast buying behaviour, and demographics is not the place to start from. A product offering must be for today, not for some time in the future. Doctor Flux is always at work, changing things in little ways and big ways and making sure that you do not accurately predict the future. By the time you get to 80 you might be back at college, full time, taking a degree course and competing with 20 year old classmates in the pole vaulting event.

In using secondary research you must make assumptions based on the data to arrive at a decision to act. The raw data must be accurate and timely – in fact time is of the essence. As people are constantly changing, old data is no data. Then the data has to be interpreted and converted into information. Once upon a time I bought a list of prospective (domestic) customers from the most reputable list supplier I could find. Having sent out a mail shot to each individual, my telesales team then telephoned the prospects. In 35% of the calls the listed person no longer lived at the address given by the list supplier. The data supplied to me converted into very poor information, was at least several years old, and over one-third inaccurate. Consequently, one-third of my team's time and effort was wasted.

If things have changed since the data was gathered it will simply mislead you. Be aware, also, that you will not use all the data available to you. You will select the data that you want, and by doing so you will have excluded the rest. You will have compounded the inaccuracies in the data by putting a boundary around your rational thinking which, in turn, will exclude the possibility of some outcomes. Even worse, you will never know which outcomes you locked out of your world.

You have effectively made at least part of your final decision when you select the data. The first step in the process of thinking logically is the primary stage, when you select the input data. The second stage is when you draw conclusions, maybe several options, from the data. This second stage is the attractive stage of thinking because the limitations you have imposed on the data have narrowed down the problem and made it less scary. You can easily convince yourself that you are using logic. Most people pay attention to second stage thinking, ignoring or hurrying through the primary stage.

The third stage is making the final decision. It will appear that you have made a logical decision based on the data. Your apparently logical assumptions, options and conclusions may be based on garbage in, garbage out. All is not lost; there is something to salvage. If anybody asks you why you made that decision, whether it subsequently turns out to be right or wrong, you have composed a perfect rationale that provides a perfect answer. One that will make it clear to others that you are not insane and neither are you stupid. That will make you feel better, since you can choose to believe it as well. Anyway, many companies go bust, not just yours.

The logic of demographics is seductive but there is another very sound reason for not putting too much faith in easily predictable future trends. Everybody with the slightest interest in marketing is almost drowning in a cascade of demographic data and analysis. So, if you think that you can outrun all the others that have exactly the same access to the data as you have, then maybe you should reconsider your approach. Else, it could be a Battle Royale.

It might be like Henry V and Agincourt all over again. As the French knights advanced through the mud into the apex of a triangle formed by the terrain, they kept going until they started to fall over each other. The weight of their armour, combined with the suction of the mud, meant that they could not get up. Most of them died, not from the skill of the English archers, but from blows to the head by the English soldiers. Too much armour can kill you, especially if the decision to wear it is taken before the day of the battle and when the information about the terrain was derived from last year's experience.

The following small article appeared in *The Times* (London, Nov 11 2006):

"A survey this week revealed another win for healthy nosh in its battle with junk food. It compared people's opinions towards food and lifestyle with those of five years ago, and not only do fewer people believe that health food is solely for pale-looking people in sandals, but more of us think that all fast food is junk food."

A few lines later:

"Although 6 per cent more people believe their diet is very good, there is an annual 10% rise in obesity."

Doesn't that immediately convince you of the value of market research? People are saying one thing to the researchers and doing exactly the opposite.

Primary research is when you engage in your own market research, focused on what you want to find out. When you are starting up a new company you are faced with an intrinsic difficulty. You cannot do real market research for something that is new and not yet on the market. As many of the largest companies in the world discover.

"MacDonald's Arch Deluxe, an adult-taste burger failed on launch despite positive results from market research". (Matt Haig, *Brand Failures*, Kogan Page, 2003, p.31). "We would love an adult burger," they enthused. But they didn't show up to buy it. MacDonalds is one of the most well-known and respected brands in the world (alternatively trading first and second place, in international recognition, with Coca Cola). They have a lot more resources than a small start-up company and can afford to employ the best market researchers. Yet they got it completely wrong. Wouldn't it be a little naïve to assume that you can do better market research than MacDonalds? Formal market research doesn't work very well when dealing with qualitative research. Sure, it can count heads and tell you that there are 25,000 people aged between 16 and 30 living in your catchment area. But it cannot predict their behaviour. Maybe, when the researchers asked Joe Public if he would buy an adult burger, they got an enthusiastic 'yes' from most people. But Joe probably thought that 'adult' was something to do with sex. It is difficult to design a foolproof questionnaire.

To engage in primary research before you start up your company means that you have to make assumptions. You will have to make an assumption about what your product offer is, exactly. No changes allowed later; that would negate all the research. You will have to make an assumption about the composition of your market. You will have to define the customers' qualities that you consider relevant and define the geographic area in which you are going to trade. If you change customer types later, all the research that you have done is invalidated. If you decide to operate within a different geographic area you will also make your primary research redundant.

The following real-life examples of what can happen are taken from my own experience whilst advising companies.

When Eve's Events launched their company they offered management of a wide range of events, targeted at the corporate market. In particular, they defined their market segments as banks, large firms of solicitors and advertising agencies, in the geographic area of Greater London. They advertised widely on the web, with keywords including 'extreme sports', murder mystery dinners, product launches and parties of all sorts. They used listings in Yell.com and Talking Pages. They also used a direct mail campaign to their target segments.

They launched the company and immediately scored a bull's eye. The first product out of the gate was a party for an advertising agency. This job was gained by personal contact – a friend of one of the directors was a director of the advertising agency. The second product out of the gate was extreme sports, booked by individuals, mostly young men. The third product was children's birthday parties, booked by wealthy parents.

To date, they have not gained another event from an advertising agency and have never got an order from a bank or large firm of solicitors.

However, they are doing extremely well producing birthday parties for individuals of all ages. Best of all, they have picked up several large retail companies who have become regulars, with two or more major events every year from most of these customers.

The mistake they made was to make assumptions about the composition of their market area and their customer types. This mistake was countered by the fact that they advertised widely, not just to their target segment and they listened to the market feedback. In effect, they did not get out there and find customers. The customers – the market – found them.

Oak Tree Plumbing started in a garage and launched by offering a plumbing service to householders, primarily repairs and maintenance. As the business grew, stocks of materials grew and they moved to retail premises (in a secondary position). They took advantage of the retail site to offer bathrooms and showers for sale to retail customers. Within a few years they were the market leader in shower equipment in their catchment area, a large proportion of sales coming from builders and plumbers. The market segment had broadened and the product supplied had changed. This was not part of their original idea. They took advantage of their physical resources and reacted to what the market was asking for.

So, instead of having a carefully worked out plan that is set in stone, just work out a marketing promotions mix as best you can and just try it and see. Offer the product widely to begin with and the market will find you. As soon as it does, you will know where you are going (probably). We will come back to this in the Reactive Phase, in much more detail.

Some people, fortunately not many, spend months and months fiddling about with market research, in the vain hope that it will provide answers that will remove the risk from the new business venture. Frequently they end up suffering from a form of repetitive brain injury called paralysis by analysis.

If you are inclined to do all this research and then write it all up in a large and impressive marketing plan, you will find what military men have always known: no plan survives contact with the enemy. When you launch your product you will find, in practice, all your research and planning documents stay in the bottom drawer as reality bites you on the ass. But you will be alive and participating in the real world and that is the exciting, even exhilarating, thing about running your own business. Pour me another small glass of adrenaline, please. Stirred, but not shaken.

Customers are different from each other, sometimes in big and obvious ways, sometimes in subtle ways. Consequently, the ideal way to sell to your customers is on a one-to-one basis, a 'relational marketing' format. In that way, you can find out exactly what each individual needs and wants, in terms of the types of products and the nature of the service preferred. You can also determine to which selling approach they are most receptive. The downside of the one-to-one selling approach is that it is a very expensive operation.

For instance, there are many small builders' merchants, each surviving on maybe as few as 40 regular customers, usually small builders and maintenance departments of large companies. It is common for the merchant, as an individual, to form relationships with each of these builders and secure and hold their regular custom. If each of these builders spends $200,000 each year, then the merchant has captured sales revenue of $8,000,000, plus revenue from irregular 'walk-ins'. The merchant does not need to advertise or engage in any form of marketing other than maintaining personal relationships with the builders. The golf club and the country club will provide nests of potential customers.

This type of business, one based on personal selling by the boss, has the disadvantage that it finds it difficult to grow beyond the stage of about 40 personal customers. It tends to stay as a 'simple form' business, with a structure consisting of two layers – the boss and the workers. This type of business can only exist where each customer brings a considerable amount of repeat business.

The personal relationship between supplier and customer means that it can be exploited, by the customer, in respect of pricing. "Joe's prices for four-by-two timber, planed all round, is a bit less than yours" said the customer. "Maybe you can drop down to match his prices?" When the question is asked on the green at the 16th hole, what option has the builders' merchant? He cannot afford to lose the customer to his competitor; he's only got 40 customers. The boss will always make a living from this type of company, but he is never likely to be very rich because it is a price-sensitive business format. Delegation does not happen and, if the boss suffers from a long-term illness or dies, so does the company.

Most companies do not have customers that spend a great amount on a regular basis. They need many more customers than 40, maybe many thousands. Consequently, the company personnel cannot form personal relationships with all their customers and mass marketing must be adopted. This will include branding, where the relationship is formed between the individual customer and the brand itself. Imagine that you went to buy your regular Gillette shaving cream and the shop assistant said that Gillette had asked them not to sell it to you! It would create an emotional reaction akin to being dumped by a previously loyal friend.

Mass marketing is expensive due to the costs of mass promotions, including advertising. All customers are treated the same and there must be a sufficient number of target customers to justify the marketing spend. It follows that the company must have the capacity to process and deliver huge quantities of the products or services.

It is possible that your start-up company will be somewhere between the mass market model and the personal sales model. Within the thousands of potential customers that you could make contact with you will find that there are groups of similar customers, with similar needs and desires. They may also allow you to treat them the same when using your marketing methodology. There may be more than one of these market segments that you want to deal with and which may require an entirely different methodology from others. Beware of trying to run what would effectively be two companies at this start-up stage. In the next chapter we shall dig into market segmentation in more detail.

Chapter 7

The World According to...

We are still in the pre-start, Analytic Phase and need to construct the framework for the world within which you are going to play. If 'all the world is a stage', then think of this as the scenery on the stage, the auditorium size, where it is going to be and the nature of the audience.

In the last chapter we considered three different ways of approaching the customer, depending on their numbers. We looked at personal one-to-one relationships for small numbers, brand relationship for large numbers and segmentation for middle of the road numbers. Assuming that you want to grow your business beyond the personal relationship level then the best approach is to consider the segmentation approach. Even if you have the start-up wealth to support mass marketing, it would be a mistake to start out that way, as the subsequent growth phases will demonstrate. The *Titanic* should definitely have done a test run before investing so heavily.

What constitutes a viable market segment? Bearing in mind that you are considering selling to a segment of the market rather then the whole mass market, your objective can be to minimise your initial investment, in terms of fixed assets, working capital and overheads. Although smaller than the mass market, the segment must be of a size sufficient to allow you to generate enough sales revenue to cover your costs and make a profit. The two key elements of the segment are that the segment members must all be inclined to buy the same product or product range, and that they are all receptive to the same marketing approach. Other than those two requirements your segments can be constructed as you feel appropriate.

For example you might select by age group or sex or income or geographical location or whatever. To allow you to decide whether you have selected a coherent and viable segment the following criteria might be helpful. Most companies have a number of segments available to choose from, which is just as well. As we have seen, it is not unusual for companies to start out with a particular segment in mind and then be forced, or enticed, to change to another segment. Before starting up, it might be helpful to identify as many different segments as possible, viable ones that you feel you can serve profitably. It's OK to pick groups that you already know, that you like, or with whom you share some degree of familiarity. A viable segment is viable only if it conforms to certain criteria, which we shall now discuss.

The segment members, those that make up the segment, must be identifiable. That seems pretty obvious, as otherwise you wouldn't know who they are or where to find them. But here is a real life example from a company selling home fabrics. They defined their segments as professional type women:

- 36 to 55, with children; values "feminine style", "comfort"
- 20 to 35, single, values "home as sanctuary and comfort zone"
- 56+, (grand-)mother, values "traditional"

Apart from the age, it would be impossible for a shop assistant to identify them; it would be impossible for a marketing person to mail them with an invitation to a fashion show. They cannot be identified without considerable cost and it is debateable whether their 'values' could ever be truly identified.

Conversely, a supplier of tools defined their segment as "tradesmen; specifically plumbers, carpenters, electricians, bricklayers, plasterers and decorators". Most tradesmen who spend on tools are working for their own outfit, rather than being employed by a firm, and therefore they need to advertise. They can be located from published lists, advertisements, van signage and they tend to frequent builders' merchants. Are they identifiable by shop assistants? Mostly, yes. However, this particular tool company improved their ability to identify their target customer by offering them loyalty cards, entitling them to discounts. The cards allowed the assistants to immediately identify them from the D.I.Y. customers, and they could invite them to the spring show or introduce them to a new range of professional tools. The loyalty cards also helped to identify their historic spending pattern.

You will need a segment population large enough to justify your attention, time and financial investment. Don't just guess the numbers; count and list by name what you think would be a viable number. Check the viability with your 'stage hands', to counter your natural optimism, common at start-up time. If you are selling garden products then locate and list the roads where people apparently take an interest in their gardens, defining the numbers.

Your chosen segment members will have to be profitable, in two ways, if they are businesses. Firstly, they must be profitable in themselves, sufficiently to pay your bills on time and not to go bust whilst they owe you money. Secondly, they must be profitable to you, in that they must be prepared to pay your prices. If they spend only $50 each year, then your expenditure per head, on marketing, servicing and administration has to be pretty low. If you are preparing to sell mortgages to sub-prime borrowers, you will need to be fairly fast on your feet in laying-off your loan book to some kindly investors, preferably over 90 years of age and of unsound mind. I think they call them 'banks'.

You will need to be able to reach the segment members easily and economically for promotional purposes. You need to know what magazines and newspapers they read and what TV and radio they enjoy regularly, so that you can advertise in the appropriate media. If you want the option of using a more direct approach to your potential customers you will need to know their names, house and email addresses and telephone numbers.

If you deliver your product to them, can you recover the cost of doing so? You might have to consider the costs of dealing with offshore customers and whether their delivery costs will be acceptable.

A further judgement you will have to make is attempting to attribute a life-span to the segment. You will be better able to do this if you have some idea of the products or services that you might offer. Skateboards, sold to young men aged eight to twenty-eight, have been around for a long time, but hula hoops disappeared a long time ago. The arrival of digital photography has caused some segments to reduce in size and other, new segments, to grow.

Here is a thought for the future. If you can service the whole of the segment, and you are the first mover, you may well be able to achieve and maintain a dominant position. Copycat competitors would be faced with the problem of switching your customers to themselves, and that can be a slow and costly process for the newcomer to the market. That might become a strategic objective for your company.

Applying the above criteria to business segments is a lot easier than applying them to consumers. However, if you are producing a product that you intend to distribute by way of retailers, for instance, the following criteria might be appropriate.

The retailers must be single-outlet operations (multiples need a different marketing approach and might constitute a separate segment). They must have a minimum of 200 square feet available to display your product and space for two months back-up stock.

The retailers must be recognisable by the buyers or end users as the type of retailer that would sell your product. Selling your perfume through a hardware store will result in lower sales and lower prices, whilst a lingerie store or a beauty salon might be more effective. The location of the retailers that you select may be important here.

There must be a sufficient number of suitable retailers to justify your time and financial investment. They must be profitable in themselves, since they will expect credit if they are expected to hold stocks. A check on their trading accounts would be advisable. They must be profitable to your company, indicating that performance expectations must be agreed with them. We must ensure that they do not go bust, so we must allow them to make sufficient profit by giving them proper gross margins

The segment members must be accessible to you, in relation to deliveries and merchandising visits. An interactive website, for ordering, invoicing, payments, trading advice and assistance in respect of product benefits would be appropriate. Maybe a webcam facility to enhance the relationships between merchandiser visits.

Survival fitness of the retailer must be evidenced; no fashion fads or fly-by-nights. You might need to ascertain their trading history. If they are a very new operation, consider getting personal guarantees or, at least, apply a 'Romalpo' clause in your terms and conditions, so that, in the event of a retailer going belly-up you are legally entitled to recover your stuff (what's left of it).

Does the image of the retailer fit with the image that your company tries to portray? The location of the outlet may be important, perhaps needing a primary position on the main drag. Maybe you are positioned in the market as a less expensive product so perhaps a side street off the main drag is best. If you are very exclusive, you might want retailers only in the major fashion cities of the world. Or maybe you should be in every mall from here to Timbuktu?

In some companies that I have worked with there was a cultural behaviour pattern that treated the retailers, part of the distribution chain, as their market and their customer. Avoid this escapist error; the market is the consumer or user of the product, they are the real customer. Although you must have sales techniques to persuade the distribution chain to handle your product, it is the market of users that drives sales of the product. You need to use a 'push' marketing strategy to push your product onto the distributors' shelves, but you also need a 'pull' strategy, aimed at the end-user, to pull the product through the distribution chain. Assuming that the distribution chain handles products other than your product, the responsibility for the push and pull strategies remains with you. Sophisticated retailers will expect you to promote the product that you expect them to sell to the customer.

Many start up companies become very optimistic when they count up all the possible customers that they could approach. Usually, this is over-optimistic. The cost of promoting the product to a large number of customers is overlooked at first. Another aspect, frequently overlooked, is the number and size of existing companies that are already supplying those customers. If the market has sufficient supply to satisfy all the customers now, then something or some company has to give way if a newcomer tries to enter the market. Frequently the newcomer is the company that fails.

If the existing companies are serving the market in full, then all of the customers have a relationship with one or more suppliers. If you intend to enter the market you must switch the customers' loyalty from their existing supplier to your company. There are a few questions to ask in order to devise a way of achieving this switch. These questions are best asked of your prospective customers. At this stage, you can only have an intention as to who these customers are. Once you get started the customers might turn out to be a different bunch to those that you initially thought would be your future. Like the real life example of Eve's Events, mentioned in the last chapter. When you get some helpful answers you will be better informed and begin to narrow down your focus, by eliminating some types of customers.

If you have a segment of customers in mind and then you find that all these customers have signed a three year contract with their supplier, what are you going to do? How do you switch them? To entice a person to break a formal contract can be illegal and the enticer might be liable to pay damages. Perhaps you should ignore this lot, at least for the time being. Or determine when the contract is due for renewal & pitch in before that date.

There's another form of contract between a customer and a supplier and it isn't written down. It's called a 'relational contract' and it is an informal relationship based on confidence, trust, friendship and built by frequent transactions and many points of contact. Why should the customer switch to a stranger with whom he or she has never had any dealings? It amounts to an obvious risk, one that the prospective, rational, customer might reasonably avoid simply by staying put.

A third form of contract is the spot contract – the deal is done on the spot, with very little formality. Walk into a shop, make an offer for a shirt and, if the shopkeeper agrees to supply you, exchange money for the shirt and leave. It is all done on the spot. The terms of a spot contract are implied and are covered by the ordinary laws and customs of the place where the transaction takes place. For instance, the shirt must be 'fit for purpose' and made in a 'proper and workmanlike manner'.

Spot contract customers are *relatively* easy to switch, especially if you catch them when they have a complaint against their supplier. They can be difficult to switch if they are regular patrons of the pub or, if male, the clothes shop. If your product is one that evokes the desire for variety, you will find the customers easy to switch. However, they can switch away from you just as easily. Menu fatigue in a restaurant or poor buying in a fashion clothing store encourages customers to switch away.

Spot contract customers rely heavily on the brand image of the supplier and the customers' perception is based on their experience of the qualities of the brand. You will only get one chance, usually, to capture this switch-able customer. Advertising that says 'we are the best' evokes the customer response of 'well, they would say that, wouldn't they?' You will have to be more subtle in your approach. Wait for the Reactive Phase, starting from the next chapter, for more on marketing.

Many people starting up a new company place undue emphasis on the creation of a brand, as if without deliberately creating it they would lack a brand. As soon as the first customer experiences your product and service then you have a brand, with brand awareness limited to one potential customer. It has been created inside the mind of the customer and has acquired various qualities based on their experience. If their first contact with you was turning up at your shop at 10:30 and finding it closed, their perception will award your brand the quality of 'inconvenient, due to late opening, probably careless about their treatment of customers'. You have a brand, whether you like it or not, and it is the property of the customer who awards it to you. If you act properly in respect of the customers, it will be a positive award, like an Oscar; if you don't act in a way that pleases, they will award you the wooden spoon. Meanwhile, do not pay $1 million to a brand consultant to create a brand. The customers will do that for free.

If you find that the customers you are trying to switch to your company have very little in the way of existing options to switch into, you may have discovered a gold mine. Regardless of the nature of the contract that they have, they may feel that they are trapped, without enough choice. Adopt the bank robber's strategy: go where the money is, and go there often.

Once you have got some customers they might switch to other companies. Try to think up features, benefits and devices for your product offer that increase the switching costs of the customer. For instance, if you are trading business-to-business (B2B) consider placing one or more of your people inside your customer's organisation. The human implant is a technique used widely by travel companies, implanting into very large companies. The customer buys into the convenience which results from having an expert on hand. The customer also benefits from the comfortable feeling of having outsourced the responsibility for managing the travel department efficiently.

Using a human implant into a large company is possible even for start-up companies. To the customer, it is less trouble than hiring an employee, with less onerous contractual obligations. Just like going for a job interview, you only need to convince the customer of your competence.

You will note that 'human' precedes the word 'implant', implying that there is some other form of implant. Yes, there is. You can implant your technology into your customers' organisations. Travel companies during the 1980s implanted personal computers into their customers' organisations, allowing the PC user to switch into the travel company's exclusive software whenever they need to book a flight or a hotel or whatever. When you have this sort of convenience, it is difficult to switch away to another travel company. You can still use these techniques today, including video conferencing kit or webcams, whereby you can build better and easier contacts that become relational contracts.

When you are trading B2B into customer organisations you should try to build multi-level relationships between your company and the customer's company. By multi-level I mean relationships between you, the boss, with the boss of the customer company and relationships between your employees and the customer's employees at the same level. This can frequently prevent the common occurrence, when there is a change of buyer, of switching by the new buyer to his or her favourite suppliers. If good relationships have been built, there is an outcry by others within the customer's company if the new buyer tries to switch away from the comfort of the existing supplier – and that's you.

Selling to businesses usually needs some sort of reward for the buyer and for the moment think of the buyer as the decision maker, not necessarily the person who tells you that you have got the contract. One of the most important rewards that you can give to a buyer is job security. There used to be a saying that 'nobody got fired for buying IBM', because IBM was the dominant player in the major IT industry. The quality of top-of-the range reliability, their dominant size, linked with their long history in the business meant that they were regarded as the best. So, if the purchase failed subsequently, the buyer could say to the boss, "Well, I bought IBM and nobody could have done better than that" The boss would reply: "There, there" whilst patting the buyer on the head, "I know you bought the best and nobody can blame you"

Although you have to tread carefully with bribery and corruption, a little light entertainment is generally acceptable, especially if it is dispensed to a broad group. One of my architect clients used to do a day at the races, providing hotel accommodation and all the wining and dining for the visiting buyers. The racecourse was small, local and very pretty and the buyers were very anxious not to miss this exclusive annual event.

Some entrepreneurs enter their chosen market, in which there are very big players as perceived competitors, with considerable trepidation. This fear and trembling is seldom justified. The big players are made up of people just like you, except that they are less flexible in their actions and reactions due to bureaucratic reporting systems.

An example of the newcomer, a five man band, defeating national and international competition is described in Chapter 2. The company that devised the image handling software for architects was up against the major names that provide software for the purpose of handling images. Yet, the newcomer took the very large crocodile's share of the market with little effort and gained almost 90% market penetration against their named and sized target market. They substituted their product easily because it did less than the software offered by the international players. I'll repeat that: it did *less than* the competition's software. It omitted everything that was not of use to architects and it included features that were useful only to architects. It was a small and deadly accurate product and sold at a higher price than the generic software on the market.

The switching costs of the customers were very low. They just dumped the generic software, already paid for some time ago – a sunk cost – and substituted the new product. If your product or service can narrow down the applications already on the market it could achieve the same success.

Conversely, by improving a feature on an existing product you can begin to substitute your product for the market leaders' product. Just target the improvement at a niche market, one that the big boys will probably dismiss as not worth the bother. Thereby, you can create the breach in the market wall through which all your future products can enter.

Another young company, the directors of which had considerable experience of the off-shoring of software development, also breached the market walls with their form of substitution. Many large companies have their own internal offshoring departments. However, these departments were not subjected to any commercial pressures and, since they were not compared to any other performers, they consequently became sloppy, lazy and incompetent. In one case, a large company had two offshoring contracts in place with the same offshore supplier and they were paying double the rate for one of the contracts. Nobody within the company noticed, until it was pointed out by an outsider.

The offer to the large companies was a pitch offering to substitute for the internal department, thereby reducing costs, ensuring keen market rates for personnel and transferring the risks on completion times and quality of work. In summary: the same function, better results and less risk.

Section 3

Reactive Phase

Chapter 8

Groundhog Day

"The map is not the territory. Let's hit the ground" says Robert de Niro in *Ronin*, as they are researching their ambush of the guys who have the briefcase. So they set off to Nice and experience the layout of the terrain. Just like the riders at the Badminton Three Day Event, who walk the course before riding it, pacing the spaces between the combination jumps, working out the approaches to the complicated jumps and discovering what unexpected obstacle awaits them on the other side. This is so much more effective, in terms of information gathering, than merely studying the map of the course.

The Reactive Phase of business growth is the time when you have to start trading and reality begins to bite you on the backside. You are now past the stage when secondary research can be of any use to you and it is necessary to switch completely to conducting primary research. Primary research is research that has never been done before; or, if it has, the results are not available to you.

Primary research, if contracted out, also means that the information coming back to you is filtered by others. There is an advantage available to you in that the information received by you from the contractor may not have the same bias that you would have put on it. In that way, it may give you other, more useful, perspectives on the product market qualities. Unfortunately, sometimes the external agency is aware of the 'shoot the messenger' phenomenon and will determine your expectations beforehand and then tailor the information to accord with your expectations. It is a brave agency that reports back to you that all your ideas are complete garbage and should be binned.

Be very much aware that, in carrying out your own research, you will have a natural human tendency to find evidence that reinforces beliefs that you already hold firmly in your psyche. This will be more apparent if you have preferred outcomes in respect of the research. You will treat evidence that supports your preferences more favourably than evidence that contradicts them. You must engage others to advise, like the stage hands mentioned earlier, to deliberately introduce perspectives that are different from your own. Encouraging these advisers and helpers to dispute with you and argue against you might be irritating at the time, but may well be to your advantage in the immediate and long-term future. Ask questions and extract their ideas for solutions and opportunities.

Your customers, your products and the relationship between them form the essence of your business. You must engage directly with your customers and not delegate it completely to other members of staff. This should be your primary task at the beginning of this phase of growth.

If you are tempted to produce a questionnaire, forget it quickly. Every question that you include in a questionnaire will be loaded with your predisposed beliefs, biases and prejudices. Unconsciously, you will formulate questions that have built-in assumptions and which exclude otherwise possible answers, and you will tend to include assumptions that confirm what you wish was true.

Once, in a relatively large organisation, I saw the results of a staff questionnaire which was quite revealing. The formulation of the questionnaire had been delegated to the recently appointed Marketing Director and one of the questions posed was: 'To what extent did you understand the content of the marketing plan?' The answer was to be expressed as a percentage and the reported result was 85% (mean average) understanding by the staff. A very satisfactory result, one might think. However, at the time that the staff survey had been conducted, the marketing plan had not yet been completed and had not been circulated. No member of staff except, presumably, some in the marketing department had seen a copy.

Did the staff deliberately lie? Possibly, if they thought that they might have been the only person who had not read the marketing plan and might face some criticism in those circumstances. Alternatively, they might have thought that they had actually read the plan, simply because they wanted to believe that they had done so. They might have listened to some marketing people talking informally about part of the content of the plan and persuaded themselves that was sufficient for them to understand the plan. After all, they wouldn't know that there was a lot more of the plan to understand, if they had no knowledge of the whole plan.

Talking with a few people, face to face, is better than analysing hundreds of written questionnaires. Talking with people allows you to understand them, at least to a better extent than is possible from reading written questionnaires. Some communications people say that words form only 5% of communication – the rest is body language and tone of voice.

There is a film, directed by Harold Ramis and released in 1993, called Groundhog Day which is set in a little town in Pennsylvania called Punxsutawney. Each year, towards the end of the winter, the people of the town gather to see the elders of the town engage with the groundhog. If the groundhog wakes after its winter slumber and sees a shadow, then "we got six more weeks of winter"

In the film, Bill Murray plays the part of the irritable and egocentric weathercaster Phil Connors, who is really pissed off by having to cover this annual festival, which he feels is personally demeaning and ridiculous. On the morning of Groundhog Day he wakes at six o'clock to the sound of his radio alarm blaring out '*I got you, babe*'. Phil, the weatherman rises and, in a bad mood, sets off to deliver his straight-to-camera coverage of the great event. He bumps into a man on the landing, exchanges a few irritable words, is short-tempered with his landlady and ostentatiously ignores the poor man begging on the street corner. He meets Ned, an old school friend, whom he brushes off in a brusque manner and then steps off the pavement into a large puddle of water.

Phil delivers his commentary piece in a begrudging manner, much to the annoyance of the cameraman and his producer, Rita, played by Andie MacDowell. Phil wants to get the hell out of Punxsutawney as quickly as possible and head for home. However, a snow storm blocks the roads and they all have to stay another night in town.

The following morning Phil wakes at six to the sound of his radio alarm: '*I got you, babe*'. He rises, goes to the window and sees the ground is still covered in snow, as it was the previous morning. He leaves his room and bumps into the same man as yesterday, engages in irritable behaviour, which is exacerbated further by his landlady asking the same questions as she did yesterday. He asks what day it is and he is told that it is Groundhog Day. But that was yesterday, wasn't it? But no, it can't be. He hurries on, ignores the pleas of the beggar, meets Ned, is equally short with him and again steps in the puddle of water.

This scenario continues and he wakes at six the next day – '*I got you, babe*' – and continues to have the same experiences. Except that he now knows where the puddle is and moves to avoid it. As the days go by, due to experience, he starts to predict events. He begins to alter his behaviour in relation to the beggar, to Ned, and even starts to treat Rita in a more kindly manner. In fact, as he learns more about Rita every day he impresses her with his apparent compatibility. Whilst he remembers the events of the previous day, she is completely unaware that she has given him information about herself.

Eventually, he learns almost everything about Rita and feigns compatibility with her love of 19c French poetry, pretends that his favourite drink is Sweet Vermouth on the rocks – the same as hers – with a twist, and that the salutation on knocking it back is 'to world peace'. As he continues to feign compatibility with Rita, it becomes real and they fall in love.

It is only when he loses his egocentricity and begins to take an interest in other people that his behaviour changes. If he does things differently, others respond differently, opening the doors to new possibilities. If he does not alter his behaviour to suit others, nothing changes. At the end of the film they decide to get together and stay in Punxsutawney. "Let's live here. We'll rent to start" Rent to start, because Dr Flux is still in action and don't invest in buying a house until you are sure that there is stability in the relationship.

In your business you will find yourself in Punxsutawney and it will be Groundhog Day over and over again. But each day you will be learning more and more and when things don't work well, you will change your behaviour and your assumptions about others. You will engage in conversations with potential customers, discovering their likes and dislikes and their patterns of behaviour, all in relation to your business. You will begin to predict the behaviour of your customers. This sounds very comforting, but you can never relax in exploring the needs and desires of your customers.

The more you experience your customers' behaviour, the better you will become at anticipating their requirements. But you must always continue to engage first hand with you customers. Predicting the future from experience is called 'induction' – you induce their future behaviour from the patterns of behaviour that you observed previously. Induction is a valid method of predicting human behaviour only providing that the world stays the same.

For instance, when Joe walks into his regular bar every evening, the discussion with the barmaid is limited to "The usual, Joe?" "Yes, please, Josephine" Josephine can predict the customer's behaviour. I visited a hostelry recently, which I had not been back to for about 10 years; the regular Joes that I knew had all moved on and were no longer frequenting that bar. With a 10 year gap, the changes are obvious, but less obvious when you are in the thick of it and the changes are happening slowly. It is not sufficient to get to know your customers and conclude that their behaviour will stay the same for long periods of time. Your close engagement with them must be life-long. One evening Joe will walk into the bar, to be greeted by Josephine's "The usual, Joe?" and the reply will be "Not tonight, Josephine"

In the film Groundhog Day, Phil Connors is collecting information from Rita for use the next day and he echoes what she says about her sweet tooth. Phil says, within her hearing, "Doesn't like fudge, white chocolate". Rita hears, takes offence, and slaps his face. When engaging with customers it must be remembered that it is not a war; it is a seduction and the approach and the understanding must be subtle. Making written lists of what people like and dislike is too crude. You need to be subtle enough to 'feel' not so much what they want, but the *sort* of things that they want. It is easy to trap yourself by being too prescriptive.

Companies that come to a standstill in the Reactive Phase, stay there because they are egocentric and do not take the time or make the effort to understand and relate to their customers. They substitute internal performance criteria in place of external criteria and internal targets become the objectives of all strategies and tactics. An obvious symptom of the malaise is that management meetings concentrate on analysing the management accounts whilst completely ignoring product and market information. Many companies that I know well have been in that state for many years, always struggling to maintain sales revenue simply by setting targets 10% higher than the previous year. This represents more of a wish list than an action list.

As an example of what can be achieved, one company took my advice to put some focus groups together, using a specialist agency. It had to be done that way because the directors could not bring themselves to engage with the lowly customers. The focus groups, professionally facilitated, elicited the most obvious shortfalls in product features and in communications. The outcome of the focus group research was extraordinarily powerful.

The entire range of products was redesigned in the light of the focus groups' comments. The publicity graphics were redesigned, photos re-shot, quality control systems instituted and, down the line, the independent retailers were offered more time and support. Having crept along, in line with inflation for the previous eight years, the next five years showed a sevenfold increase in sales revenue.

Before we leave the groundhog to go back to sleep in Punxsutawney, there is perhaps one more metaphor that could be drawn out. When Phil Conners, the weatherman, arrives in Punxsutawney his objective is to do his straight-to-camera piece as quickly as possible and then get the hell out of there. However, due to Dr Flux and the changing world about him, he changed his behaviour and a further consequence was that his *objective* changed to 'the seduction of Rita'. And he ended up in a much better place than he could have foreseen when he first arrived to report on the groundhog weather forecast. Now buy or rent the film, watch it and enjoy it and allow the metaphors to sink into your mind and become part of your learning.

Many start-up companies set out with an objective to sell to a market segment which they have defined before market testing. Many fail to sell to their predefined target segment and the company itself fails. Others do change their behaviour and take what comes to them, and make a success with an entirely different market segment. Along the way, the product is also modified to suit the new segment.

One of the expressions used in marketing is that of 'marketing leakage'. It is used to describe the leaking of promotional information from the intended target market to other market segments. For example, an engineering firm selling spare parts to automobile repair shops might advertise in specialist automotive magazines that are also read by car club enthusiasts. This marketing leakage might attract the members of these clubs, who then try to place orders directly with the engineering firm. As it is very likely that the engineers can get a much higher price from the car club enthusiasts than is paid by the professional repair workshops, it might turn out to be a very profitable new market segment.

Not only do the engineers get a higher price, they can target not just single outlets, but nests of many customers by encouraging the officials of the clubs to circulate the marketing information to their members. Marketing cost per $ sale should be substantially lower than costs of marketing to repair shops.

Until you have proved, in practice, that you are targeting a profitable segment, allow for marketing leakage. Do not be coy and hide away from the world. Use keywords on your website that will be meaningful to a wide cross-section of potential customers. Initially, avoid advertising and promotions that are too tightly focused on a market segment that has not yet proved itself to be profitable. Rent to start; you might not like your first choice of where to settle down.

There are two ways of learning: the first is by imitating others; and the second is by trial and error. Throughout the Reactive Phase we are learning and we are doing so through trial and error, avoiding the copy-cat trap. We are, as far as we know, going where no man has gone before. Even to the extent of using split infinitives in our writing.

Imitation learning is copying what other people do and we know what they say they do through hearing what they say, reading what they write and observing their behaviour. Frequently, if you investigate the matter, you will find that many people write, but do not really believe what they write or are simply repeating something that others have written. You will find that, in a relaxed moment, they orally admit that what they wrote wasn't quite true or that they embellished it a little to make it more palatable for the reader. You will certainly get more accurate information about 'how do you do it' from relaxed conversation than you will get from the written word.

But, even in conversation, there will still be plenty of favourable embellishments to their accounts of their achievements. Phrases such as 'Do what I say, not what I do' and 'One rule for the rich, another for the poor' are popular in pointing out the fallacies that the more important persons impose on the less important. When you are starting out in business you will find plenty of these people about.

The best way of learning by imitation is to watch someone in action. Real live action that is not simulated for the benefit of an audience. If you think about it, you couldn't possibly learn to play tennis well without watching some top class tennis players.

However, the real learning comes when you get out there and do it. When, for the first time, you pick up a tennis racket and serve, it will not be an ace making a beautiful curve and pitching perfectly on the line. You are going to have to try and try and try again and again to become even a passable tennis player. If you have a coach, or two, you will be able to avail yourself of feedback, which will speed up the learning process.

But the question, in relation to the performance of your company is: what are we learning; or better, what *should* we be learning during the Reactive Phase? We are learning about our customers and about our competitors, our suppliers, our bankers, our business advisers and other stakeholders. (By stakeholders I mean anybody who has an interest in our business or who can influence our business, for better or worse.)

The primary learning objective must be to know our customers and our potential customers. We must understand their beliefs, their cultural attributes, their rituals and practices. We must observe and learn their habits; we must get to know them as if they were our closest friends. We must know them to the extent that we can create a difference, from our competitors, in our offer, a difference that is valued by our customers. Ideally, such a difference should not be capable of being fully understood by our competitors. A simple difference in product that can be reverse engineered and copied by the competitors is insufficient to gain anything more than a short-term lead in the marketplace.

Our objective in engaging in all this time-consuming learning is to be able to communicate with our customers and to make it easy for them to communicate with us, the people of the company. This will allow us to pitch our offer to them as a product that will satisfy them, whilst using the most acceptable means of delivery and communication. If we cast our net wide enough to start with, then we will be able to observe real market segments, decide on those we want to address, concentrating on them and ignoring the others.

Chapter 9

Back to the Future

There is no end of people trying to predict the future. This includes fund managers, astrologers, bank rate aficionados, horse racing punters, roulette players, company executives, Wizards of Oz and soothsayers and Delphic oracles of every description.

G.K. Chesterton was of the opinion that those people who tried to predict the future, in these times, did not use the entrails of birds, as did the forecasters of Ancient Rome. He suggested that they simply took something that was going on now and said – predicted – that it would go on some more and more until something extraordinary happened. In a sense, he was suggesting that we go back to the future. We identify trends in the past and predict that they will continue, until there is a bifurcation, a breakdown and forking of the trend. Nobody ever knows when this bifurcation (or multi-furcation) will take place or what the nature of it will be.

How would you like to make friends and influence people by demonstrating your extraordinary powers of accurately forecasting the weather? In the United Kingdom, an area which has a wide range of weather conditions and frequent changes thereof, you can be remarkably accurate. All you have to do is forecast that tomorrow's weather will be the same as today's weather. You will be right about 80% of the time. Impressive, huh?

The procedure for forecasting the future is to observe what is happening now, determine whether or not it has been happening for some time – a trend or pattern – and then forecast that it will continue to happen in the future. However, to retain your credibility, do not attempt to forecast the extraordinary event that breaks the trend or pattern.

In the context of our business, what do we want to know about the future?

Probably the most valuable forecasting in your business is to be able to predict human behaviour. Remember, also, that you and your people are human and your previous behaviour has had an effect on your customers' behaviour. If previously you did nothing in relation to your customers, then they will be behaving in a particular way, in the absence of your influence. Like in the film 'Back to the Future', when you go back and observe what is happening, you may be able to change the future.

If we are to be able to say, when they enter our sphere of operations, "The usual, Joe?", and receive an affirmative reply, then we have succeeded in our learning. We have begun to predict the customers' behaviour. Without raising your hopes too much, there are ways of predicting human behaviour. There are three ways that prediction can be achieved, described as follows.

Here's a scenario: you are sitting in Starbuck's, having a coffee and idly looking out through the window at the passers-by. On the pavement a man stops, takes out his wallet and fumbles around inside. Accidentally, he drops a $100 bill on the sidewalk.

I predict that you will predict that the man will retrieve the $100 bill before moving on. You make your prediction on the basis that, if you were him, you would retrieve the $100 bill. It just seems to you that the man would have to be nuts not to do so. Your prediction would, almost certainly, be right. In turn, my prediction of your prediction – your thought behaviour – is also almost certainly correct. This is so because, if I were you, sitting in Starbuck's, I would have made the same prediction.

Throughout the world a $100 bill is of value to virtually every adult. As we discussed earlier, money enables us to satisfy very basic human needs and desires. To a poor person it represents satisfaction of basic survival needs. To a rich person it represents power and control of his life including the control of hotel staff or a small present for a loved one or a charitable donation. We assume, quite rightly that, like us, others place a value on a $100 bill.

By proposing extreme circumstances, one can easily predict behaviour, such as predicting which way the thirsty man in the desert will go, given a choice between a bottle of water and a blanket. If I was him I would... In the real life world of the growing company the 'If I was him I would...' prediction model results in the stagnation or demise of a very large number of small companies.

In one particular case, a young woman marketing manager, in a company selling an electrical installation service to construction engineers, never, ever met or otherwise personally engaged with the customers. She used the 'If I were him...' model to design and implement all the promotional materials and used direct mail marketing tactics. After two years in post, the company had a beautiful brochure and beautiful personal cards, but sales had dropped by 8% in $ terms. The disparity of needs and wants and desires of the customers and the assumptions of the marketing manager were a million miles apart.

The bane of a business adviser's life is the creative inventor. We tend to meet them at social gatherings and when they find out that we do for a living, we end up pinned against a wall or backed into a corner. Without an eagle-eyed hostess recognising your 'I want to escape' signals, your day is completely ruined. Invariably, the inventive would-be businessman has invented a new gizmo that will solve a number of problems. The inventor's point-of-view is only his own – 'If I were them I would love this product; I would immediately appreciate its efficacy and rush to the nearest store to buy one'. Inventors get terribly depressed when you tell them that they are probably a little biased in favour of their projected gizmo and that the rest of the world may not be all that enthused by the new product. That's why I get stuck in the corner. I just can't bear the thought of all these inventors jumping off the tops of high buildings immediately after they have met me at a social gathering at what's-her-name's house.

There is another way of predicting human behaviour and it is called 'the intentional stance'. This is a concept developed by Dan Dennett, the philosopher, in a book called *The Intentional Stance*.

If a very large man, with a frown on his face and glaring eyes, approaches you head on and has an axe raised in his right hand, you will conclude from his stance that he has the intention of killing you. Replace the man with a vicious-looking tiger and you would attribute the same intention to the wild animal.

Humans all have similar basic desires which we take for granted. Humans need to survive and they need to reproduce and they intend, generally speaking, to continue to adopt that intentional stance. Humans need water, food, shelter and security. They (most of 'em, anyway), need the company of other human beings, and many engage in competition in relation to their fellow humans. Competitive elements include sports, crosswords, card games, displays of dress, possessions and even the address where they live; status is a form of competition.

We can therefore attribute intentions to other human beings. Mind you, we can also attribute intentions to inanimate objects. I know that my virtual video recorder on my computer is malignant and is out to get me. Because it is vicious and nasty, I know that it intends to freeze the screen about ten minutes before the film ends. In consequence, I verbally abuse that nasty piece of software in a futile attempt to change its intentional stance.

We can accurately predict that every human we meet or see has the intention of eating something nutritious at sometime today. We can further conclude that they are growing or storing some foodstuff, animal or vegetable, or they are going to steal or beg some food or they will buy some food today. So, if we can site a business where there are a lot of people, but no food supplies, we can create a profitable company offering almost any sort of food. Based on our prediction of human behaviour in relation to their intention to eat every day, we could grow rich.

This is what we do whenever we test-market a new product or use a new marketing process. We assume an intentional stance on the part of the potential customer and we launch on that basis. If we are wrong, we learn that this is not the way to do it because we have attributed the wrong intentional stance to the potential customers. But we learn and we react to the feedback and we do something different next time. Eventually we will get it right; if we don't, we die. The question is: have we got sufficient time and money to keep going until we find, by trial and error, the right mix to bring in the paying customers?

The intentional stance methodology for predicting customers' behaviour is somewhat inaccurate in relation to the exactitude necessary to seduce a customer segment. Except in a retail trade we have no knowledge of individual customers and, therefore, no clues that allow us to refine the intentional stance.

In retail, the business person is on the front line and engages directly with people entering the store. For example, in a fashion shoe store, a twenty-something woman enters. What intentions can we attribute to her? She might be window-shopping in her lunch hour, idly seeking what exciting new stuff might be about; or she might be comparing prices against other shoe shops. She might be sussing out the shop to determine its comfort level to include in her options for her future purchases; in which case she will evaluate, consciously or unconsciously, the layout and design of the shop and merchandise. She will make judgements on the quality and nature of the shop assistants and their attitude to customers like herself.

But supposing a 45 year old man enters the fashion shoe shop. We might reasonably conclude that he is not going to try on a pair of peep-toe, sling-back, white mid-courts. In the absence of other indicators, we might properly assume that he is a competitor and predict that he will check out our prices and presentation in order to better us.

In one retail company I set up a fun competition requiring the shop assistants to predict what a customer was going to be interested in before they entered the shop. After a little practice, they could get it right very nearly 100% of the time. When you constantly interact directly with customers, you can get well beyond the basic intentional drivers and refine down to products and processes that suit them.

If we consider our customers as a community and we wish to join that community we will adjust our behaviour to accord with the behaviour that the community exhibits. Otherwise we will be considered different and therefore excluded. We learn the rules of any community we wish to join, in order to be accepted. We used an example a little way back in respect of the barmaid in a pub predicting the behaviour of a regular: "The usual, Joe?" All day long we adjust our behaviour to fit in with people around us because we have learned to do so by constant interaction with the people with whom we engage. We learn what their behaviours are and the more we engage with them the more we can predict their behaviour. This process is called 'induction'; you will find that word used more commonly in relation to a new arrival at a company. They go through a process of induction in order to understand the behaviours required of them.

It is absolutely necessary to mix with your customers on a regular basis if you want to design the products and the processes which they will happily accept from you.

We have based our methodology for predicting customers' future behaviour on our 'Back to the Future' scenario – what has been happening and what is happening now, will continue to happen in the future. From a practical point of view, that is the best we can do. But we know that Dr. Flux never sleeps – he is always active and we need to be alert to the changes that are relevant to our business. We cannot forecast these changes accurately (nobody can), but we can observe them soon after the change takes place and react to them quickly.

There's a film, directed by Elia Kazan, called 'Gentleman's Agreement', in which Gregory Peck acts the part of a feature writer for magazines. A New York publisher commissions him to write a series of articles on anti-semitism, with the injunction to "go right to the source". So, Gregory Peck ponders and thinks 'What must a Jew feel about this thing?' He tries to write to his army buddy, David Goldman (who is Jewish), to ask him what his views are, but he thinks this might be insulting, as well as being a bit trite. Then he remembered that he had done an article on the Okies (Steinbeck's 'Grapes of Wrath' stuff, poverty-stricken people from Oklahoma making the trek to California to make their fortune).

He says, to himself, "When I wanted to find out about a scared guy in an old jalopy on Route 66, I didn't stop someone and ask a lot of questions: I bought an old jalopy myself. I lived in their camps; I ate what they ate. I found the answers in my own gut, not somebody else's. I didn't say 'What does it feel to be like an Okie. I was an Okie"

He continues, "On the coal miner series I didn't do a lot of research and sit in my bedroom. I got myself a job (as a miner) and went down and slept in a shack. I didn't try to dig into a coal miner's heart; I *was* a miner" He decides that, as he is not known in New York, he will let it be known that he is Jewish and experience it for himself. So mix with your customers at every opportunity.

If you are selling to business customers you will realize that you are not selling to a company, which is merely a legal entity. You will soon discover that you are selling to a person, who is employed by the company to act as the buyer, and will do your best to impress that person with your offer. As your understanding grows, you will realize that the person who is the buyer is not all-powerful and that there are others in the company that can affect their decision to buy your product or service.

The users of your product or service, within the customer company, may have different criteria to that of the buyer. For instance, a manufacturing company had open plan offices, within which the product design team were located, along with all the other administrative staff. When the design team acquired very pretty, very classy Apple Macs on their desktops, a user uprising took place. Everybody else wanted to dump their grey, uncool, desktop PC and replace it with an Apple Mac. The company buyer had to succumb to their demands, albeit over a period of time. The person trying to sell PCs to that company had a hard time, even though he had convinced the buyer that PCs were cheaper and just as good for administrative staff.

Companies also have a Head of Finance, who is forever concerned with costs and cash-flow. Although you may convince the buyer, the finance person can act as gatekeeper and will not allow the purchase to go through, purely on financial grounds.

There will also be a Chief Executive or Managing Director somewhere, and that CEO may be the only real decision-maker in the company in terms of purchases over a specified amount. When you've made the sale and opened the champagne, you can often find that the sale does not go through because someone that you don't know has decided against it.

Other people within the customer organisation can influence whether or not the company buys your product. If you know someone working within the potential buyer company, they might be able to help you to get a foot in the door. They could even initiate a requirement for your product or enable the start of a relationship between you and the target company that would result in sales by you. It is unlikely that you will discover all the influencers of the company buying decisions. In one case, a very large and long established company wanted one of my clients to co-brand with them on a new product range to be designed and manufactured by my client. After a protracted series of meetings and discussions the large company seemed to be behaving quite irrationally and the deal fell through. Talking to some of the executives from the large company, who were a bit embarrassed, they let it slip that the project was being heavily influenced by the Chairman's wife, who had no formal position in the company and no experience of such deals.

Perhaps you are now realizing how close you must be to your business customers and not just to one individual.

My solution to this problem is to deliberately set out to create multi-level relationships between members of your company and those of the target company. That means that several people from your company get friendly with several people from the other company. For instance, whoever collects in the money that you are owed has direct access to the buying department and the accounts department of the target company. They should find out names and engage people in friendly conversation. Eventually, they should be able to arrange meetings to discuss common processes or problems. Once relationships are established that way, then the next step is to challenge them to a game of softball in the park, with some alcoholic refreshments.

A very successful graphic design company stayed in contact with the marketing departments of many larger companies. They sponsored a 'Marketing Marathon' every summer, with a well-known charity as beneficiary, and they invited all the marketing people in their target companies to participate. All the people of the graphic design company also attended and mixed with the marketing people from the target company. When the marketing managers moved on to new jobs, the graphic design company kept in touch with them and gained a new client. When a new marketing manager arrived at the target company, the staff of the target company made sure that the friendly graphic design company continued to be the supplier of graphic design.

It is very common for senior executives to entertain other senior executives from their target companies at sporting or theatre events. Doing deals on the golf course doesn't often happen, but it enables deals to be done at a later date, off the golf course. It was popular, for a while, for executives to repeat the phrase 'lunch is for wimps'. The truth is, lunch is for forming relationships that result in sales. But remember that this practice, between executives, is insufficient in itself; it ignores the initiators and influencers and users who are lower down the organisations. These people need to be happy about your product, too; they could break a deal by objecting to it.

A small firm of architects used the technique of joining in the administration of trade bodies and managed to get elected to the committees of all the outfits that they wanted to penetrate. From their apparent positions of power, they could directly contact all the players in their product market segment and form friendly relationships with them. No mention of sales, of course. But sales sort of, emerged. They are now a very big firm of architects.

Interestingly, they monitored the number and type of events that all their senior staff attended. They encouraged and rewarded attendance, not just sales results. Meeting a person from a company stamps that company's brand on the other person. Awareness level is raised and nobody says, 'Now, what was the name of that company that did such a good job on that new development?' The company name springs immediately to mind.

Chapter 10

The Importance of Being Different

Suppose you need some bricks to rebuild part of your garden wall and, due to local planning regulations, you have to use the same type as the existing bricks. The bricks are the same wherever you buy them and you can select and order them over the internet for delivery to your door. There is no difference between suppliers or the product that matter to you. Consequently,

you shop around for prices only, giving the order to the cheapest supplier.

If you need to buy a pint of skimmed milk and all skimmed milk on offer appears to be the same, you will buy the milk that costs you less. If all the shops that you can buy milk from are equidistant from you, then you will choose the one with the lowest price. However, if one of the shops is significantly closer to you and you are in a hurry, you may pay a little more for the convenience of that difference. Likewise, if you need the milk at 10 o'clock at night, you will be prepared to pay more at the 7/11 store than you would pay at the supermarket. You have put a price on your time, trouble and exertion. The differences that matter to you here are the location of the store and the time of day.

So, you've got some nice ripe blue cheese on the cheeseboard, with some perfect apples and a few grapes for decoration. The claret glasses are gleaming next to the large, white Irish linen napkins. But you are missing something – you have no wine. So off you go to the wine store, in search of a nice red, preferably a cabernet sauvignon that will marry nicely to the cheese.

You arrive at the wine shop and inspect the wine offer, in particular the cabernet sauvignons. Now you are experiencing a little difficulty because you do not recognise any of wines; they all look roughly the same to you. How do you decide which one to buy?

You inspect more thoroughly, seeking some difference between them, but nothing significant appears to help you choose. The prices are different, but you hate buying wine by price. You look at the cheapest bottle again, rejecting it on the grounds that if it is the cheapest it is probably the least good. The most expensive seems a little over the top, so you settle for the wine that is the second lowest in price. After all, it may not be the best, but it is certainly not the worst. It would be awful to buy the most expensive wine and discover, after opening it that it was a really bad, overpriced wine. It would be an especially bad experience if it was your fellow diner who commented on your poor choice.

When all the products are much the same and the only difference is the price, the buyer will choose the cheapest. Except that, in some cases, the price also sends a signal to the buyer. In the case of the wine, the lowest price signalled that the wine was inferior. Whether or not it was inferior is not at issue; the buyer, interpreting the price signal, perceived it as being so. Buyer perception is all, and that is why signals are so important in guiding the buyers' perceptions. If the buyer was dining alone, he might well have taken a chance on the cheapest, but his fellow diner was an influencer in terms of the choice of wine.

In essence, people only buy for one of two reasons. The first reason is because the product is the lowest cost, meaning the overall cost including elements of convenience and not just the price on the label. The second reason is because the product is different and that difference is of value to the buyer. Any business must therefore create an offer that either reduces the buyer's costs, or adds value to the buyer's performance, or enhances the buyer's personal experience of the product. The coffee shop on the station concourse is in the right place and is open at the right time and can offer a choice of product. Its regular coffee will gain a price higher than other coffee shops due to its convenient location, and its product range allows for some very profitable prices on other products.

Locating a high fashion store on the Via Condotti in Rome is the place that the customer expects to find the best fashion shops and expects all of them to charge high prices for their products. The customers will pay because the products they buy will be very different, possibly exclusive, and will enhance their status when worn elsewhere or, at least, allow them to mix with the 'right' people.

Keeping your prices as low as possible may well reduce your customers' costs. I have known many a small company, with the intention of growing their business, use the strategy of lowest prices. Under-cutting the competition is the competitive advantage that they claim for themselves. I do not know them now because they have all failed and they longer exist.

The reason is fairly simple. In order to compete on price the company must have the lowest *costs*, not just low prices. In a price war, the company with the lowest costs is the last man standing. If your costs are higher than the competition, as the prices go down and down, you will start losing money before they do. Small companies cannot be the cheapest because bigger companies have greater economies of scale. Big companies can use their buying power to lower their costs of buying. They also have established processes which are probably more efficient than yours, due to their longer learning curve.

The phrase I hate most, frequently used as a signal by small companies is: "Our prices are cheaper because our overheads are smaller than our bigger competitors" Consider your photocopier or your computer set-up. Did you really buy it for less than a big company, who probably buy computers in dozens? The same photocopier is used by maybe 30 different people in a big company whilst your copier is used by only a handful of people. The big company's photocopier is many times more productive as yours, yet they only paid the same money for it, probably less, as you did. The same economies of scale apply to your office and production space, your stationary, your transport costs and just about everything else.

The choice of strategy is a choice between two. Use a 'lowest cost' strategy or a strategy of differentiation. As a small company intending to grow, you do not really have a choice. You have to use a strategy of differentiation; it is imposed on you by the existence of larger competitors. That does not mean that you can ignore the task of keeping your costs down to a reasonable level, although I have never seen a company that became successful due to cutting their overhead costs.

What is differentiation, anyway? And how can it be effectively achieved? It is the elements of the offer that you put to your customers that they place a value on, those elements that are different from the offer of your competitors. Let us look at a real-life example.

The British bathroom shop offered red lavatory seats that were imported from the USA. They were the only bathroom shop in the city that sold red lavatory seats. That's an example of differentiation, one that the customers valued and which made the company's sales increase. The red seats cost more for the shop to buy than the more common colours that had been sold for many years. However, it was easy to apply a percentage mark-up at the same rate as the old-fashioned seats. This meant that not only was the cost of the differentiation covered, but the profit was increased compared to the old seats. If the extra cost of the differentiation was only just covered, but the offer of red seats attracted more customers into the shop, then it would still have been worth it.

However, the differentiation was not sustainable. As red seats became popular the copycat competitors started to stock them. Bang went the differentiator!

However, the cunning bathroom shop stocked a popular range of chromed bathroom taps and they discovered that they could have the chrome taps lacquered in an exact shade of red to match the lavatory seats. The cost of the lacquering process was £4 and the shop added £8 to the price of the taps. This gave a further boost to sales and also increased the value of each individual transaction. As well as buying a seat, the customers also bought the matching taps. The signalling to the customer was achieved by the matching colour of the products and the exclusivity of the set – taps and seat being displayed together at the point of sale. It turned utilitarian products into exclusive fashion items and signalled to the customers that they were *expected* to pay more.

The seat and taps is an example of differentiation of the product, not in function, but in design. A similar technique worked at a national fashion shoe retailer whereby shocking pink shoes were placed in the windows, along with shoes in yellow, turquoise and other bright colours. The shoe shop didn't sell many of those, but the footfall in the shops increased appreciably and they sold many more black, brown, tan and white shoes. The signal perceived by the twenty-something customer was "Look, exciting shoes! Go on, I dare you!" The increase in sales revenue easily covered the cost of the colourful shoes.

When differentiating by product, there are some other approaches that can be used, in addition to colour. Like the loo seats and the taps, you can batch groups of products together. Clothing retailers will often display complete outfits on a shop mannequin, to encourage the customer to buy products extra to the items they intended to buy. Differences in the product can also be achieved by changing the weight, the material from which it is made, the shape and the design. You can also add features and functions, but not every product benefits by imitating the Swiss army knife – less is often more.

Product differences have an inherent disadvantage, in that the differences are visible to competitors. Consequently, they can be copied, making the differences unsustainable. The chairman of Sony, the consumer electronics multinational, is quoted as saying that their new product features have a life of only about three months, before they are copied by a competitor.

Service companies can also provide differences that are valued by their customers. The following is an example of a successful differentiator used in the provision of a service. A firm of catering equipment service engineers, having worked for a major customer for a number of years, discovered that the down time of restaurant equipment was one of the major cost elements for the client. At least that was the client's perception. The thought of the oven failing on a busy night is a bit scary for a restaurant owner and makes that event more likely, even if only in the mind of the owner. That observation was made by the service company during a number of meetings with their client. The engineers offered to reduce their customers' (possible) costs by offering a four-hour, 24/7 response time. The engineers charged more for this service and raised their prices based on the job information on downtime they had accumulated over the years. Consequently, they could calculate, fairly accurately, how to increase their prices to yield more profit. They also signalled to the buyers, simply by stating it orally, that their costs due to down time would probably be reduced.

The same engineers also signalled a high level of quality by repeatedly making it clear that they use only proprietary, branded spare parts for equipment repairs. Since copycat parts are easily available, their signal implies that they are different from competitors in that respect.

When the engineers 'signalled to the buyers' they didn't simply wave their hands in the air, whilst holding little semaphore flags. They signalled to the appropriate members of the decision making unit (buyer, gatekeeper, decision maker etc.) directly and overtly.

There are other ways of creating differentiations that are of value to the customer. You can use the stuff you buy in to create a differentiation. Notice how retailers of coffee tell you the history of the product, so that the signal you receive is 'exotic' or, in the case of Free Trade and similar the signal is 'you are a good person for buying our product. If there are too many English cheese shops in your locale, why not become an Italian cheese shop? If that's what the customer values and you are the only one, then you can charge a little more; or maybe a lot more. Country of origin can be a simple way to achieve differentiation and usually any extra cost can be covered. Would you know the relative prices of Italian and French cheeses? It is difficult to evaluate, since there are no direct comparisons. Irish butter, German engineering, Indian spices and American burgers all have intangible country of origin qualities that constitute differences for which people will pay more.

Differentiations are also to be found in the way you operate your business. We have all got quite used to Starbucks, Costa Coffee and Coffee Republic and take them for granted. But coffee shops have been around for a very long time, as Dr. Johnson's comments on 17th century coffee houses will confirm.

Immediately before the new breed of coffee shops existed, big city coffee shops were selling coffee, albeit foul-tasting stuff, in scruffy surroundings. The differences demonstrated by the new breed are the variety of coffees sold, the quality of production, cleaner and better designed premises, better locations and better trained staff. Essentially, it is the same idea as before, just much better executed. That's the difference and the higher prices obtained are the proof of its success. However, the new breed of coffee shops might find it difficult to create and sustain valuable differences between each other. It might just come down to location, location, location. Even now, as I write, the coffee shops are getting sloppy, becoming untidy and uncaring.

It is common to see new companies start up doing exactly what lots of other companies are doing. The successful ones simply do it better than the existing bunch. If better execution is your primary differentiator you will get some mileage out of it. It will take some time before competitors can decipher exactly what you are doing. It will take them even longer to copy what you do. So keep your operating manuals in a safe place and do not allow copies to get into circulation. If some of your people leave you, make sure that they leave all details of your processes and systems behind. With the boot on the other foot, I suggest you have a word with the competitors' people, over several bottles of wine, to find out the source of their differentiation.

Just in case you are getting hungry at the thought of muffins in coffee shops, we will change to something less appetising, such as body parts. In the Welcome Museum in London you will find pickled body parts displayed in glass containers, for students of anatomy and pathology to study. The same specimens (I don't mean the students), presented in the different context of an art gallery, send a signal that creates a difference of value for which customers are prepared to pay. When you consider that these specimens are bought by customers for many thousands of pounds when presented as *objets d'art*, you realise the value of signalling. Damien Hirst's shark in formaldehyde was bought for £7 million. The red taps in the bathroom shop demonstrate a similar abnormal context, albeit less dramatically. A red sweater in a clothes shop would not have attracted all that much attention. Context can be used to create a valued differentiation.

In the operations part of your business you can build differences in, for instance, reliability and consistency. To quote the *Ronseal* wood sealant advertisements, 'it does what it says on the tin'. Without stealing their strap line, many businesses could benefit from taking this position in relation to their competitors. In the food and drinks business, 'It simply tastes better', might be your differentiator. Time can be a differentiator. Who makes the longest lasting batteries? How do you know? Did you set up a test to compare them with others? In computers or food mixers or cars the differentiator could be speed, quickness, time-saving. Speed is commonly over-used as a differentiator; much of the time speed is not of value to the customer. Next day delivery is often used even for the most mundane of products; personally, I couldn't care less if the book I ordered arrives on Tuesday or Wednesday or Thursday.

Distribution systems can harbour plenty of opportunities for differentiation. How many ways can you get your stuff to your customers? By distributing from factory to wholesaler to retailer? Perhaps direct from factory to buyer? Is mail order in order for your business? Can you use the internet for better distribution of information? Maybe you can be the only company that provides a choice of delivery methods or the only one to deliver in the evenings or at weekends. A company exploiting a 'green' image uses delivery vans which, apart from the windows, lights and plates, are covered in grass!

The way you package your stuff can be different from competitors, even if it is just putting carrying handles on your boxes so that customers find it convenient to carry. Isn't it amazing how difficult some packages are to open? Try opening shrink-wrapped soft cheese without mangling the cheese. By the time I'm done it's just a soggy mess that I have to eat with a spoon.

After-sales service is another opportunity to differentiate including guarantees, physical service, availability of accessories or upgrades, credit arrangements and payment methods. Try to be really different and call your customer after every purchase to see if everything is OK. If something's wrong, you're onto something which you can correct and, having done so, your sales might grow substantially. Now that is where it really matters.

You might think that this chapter on differentiation would be more appropriately placed in the Creative Phase section. Here's an example of the reason why it appears in the Reactive Phase. Once upon a time there was a supplier who delivered to retail shops but, when the goods were delivered the shop people were faced with a problem. The packages were large and slightly too heavy for one person to carry easily. Because the packages were bulky, the supplier had bound them in steel strips, presumably for added security, in transit. The shop staff had to purchase a pair of pliers specifically to deal with these packages. In cutting the tightly bound steel strips, they sprung apart, threatening severe lacerations to the face and hands of the person opening the package. The unpleasant experience was further compounded by the internal packing, which was in the form of wood chips. On opening the package the wood chips got just about everywhere, necessitating the use of a dustpan and brush, accompanied by a vacuum cleaner. Now that's a memorable differentiation, of value to their competitors, if not to their customers!

The supplier never knew what he was doing to the shop staff because he never bothered to understand how his processes impacted on his customers. The reason this chapter is sequenced to apply after you have started trading is because you need to know your customers in order to decide on your differentiations. You must understand the context of usage of the product; how your customer actually uses it. You must also understand how every point of interaction between you and your customer impacts on the customer. What is their perception of your company? Phoning your customer after each purchase is good stuff, but you need to get to know them more thoroughly. If they are business customers then be straight down the line and tell them that you can be an even better supplier if you could walk through their processes in relation to your supply. If they are domestic customers, explain that you want to see how your product is actually used, where it's stored or if it's inconvenient in any way. You will learn more in five minutes of walkabout then you will learn from a thousand remote surveys. Jump into your customers' world; they will appreciate your interest and you can also give them a little reward.

The very best source of differentiation is the one that matters most to your customers and which is virtually impossible for your copycat competitors to decipher. The most successful differentiation comes from your people, especially when it emanates from several people. The bathroom company, the one with the red taps and loo seats, we discussed previously, had an interesting combination of people. It had probably the best salesman in the business of selling bathroom suites within its geographic area of operations. He never failed to get the sale and to please the customer. Another person who made the difference was the installation manager, a technical genius, who also had the capability to get on really well with the customers. The third part of the combination was a manager who had previously worked in high fashion in King's Road in London. That's where the state-of-the-art presentation of the bathrooms came from. During the five years they worked together there was not a single customer complaint and five years represented about 4,000 installations. Mixes of people can create some unique combinations, differentiations that are competitive advantages, whilst being indecipherable to the competitors.

A very common occurrence of people making an important difference is in the rag trade. A good fashion designer is the making of a fashion house and is the standard bearer of the brand. In fact a good designer frequently becomes a brand as valuable as the fashion house itself. Further down the fashion chain, a good buyer for a retailer is also worth their weight in gold brocade. Many a retailer has failed after the significant buyer has departed the company.

One of the reasons that 'people' can be the source of the best differentiations is that they are almost infinitely flexible and adapt to suit each customer. This obviates the need to keep on looking for new stuff, since new offers and solutions are being offered to the customers all the time. A second reason is that a product can be purchased by a competitor and yields up its secrets when subjected to a little reverse engineering. The competitor then imitates your differences. When it comes to people, the competitor will not even know who your people are, nor will they know their level of performance. Most certainly they will not be able to work out the combination that makes the essential difference. The differentiation is sustainable and confers a long-lasting competitive advantage. The bathroom company did not set out to be the market leader, but the sustainable differentiation took them to that position, which they held for longer than the five years that the managers worked together.

Recapping on the essential ingredients of successful differentiation the first point to make is that the difference must make your offer different from the competitors. To achieve this, it follows that you must know who your competitors are and how you compare. We will come to the methodology of knowing your competitors in a later chapter – it may well be new to you.

Secondly, the differences in your offer must be differences that the customers value sufficiently to allow them to buy from you, without hesitation. It follows that you must get to know your customers very well. In particular, you will need to understand their decision making unit – the people involved in the decision to buy and try to create a valuable difference for each of them.

The third important element is to understand that the customer probably will not know what differences in your offer will make a positive contribution to them. You have to keep them informed, 'them' being all the members of the decision making unit. The signals that you send must be clear and unambiguous. Only a nitwit would believe the slogan that 'We provide the best service at the lowest prices'.

The fourth thing to remember is that differentiation has a cost. You have to work out what the cost is and you have to be able to charge a price that not only covers your extra costs, but adds to your profits by increasing your gross margin.

Lastly, the differences that you offer must be sustainable over time, many years, if possible. If the differences can be copied quickly by a competitor then your advantage will disappear and your prices may well be forced downwards.

Chapter 11

Barbarians at the Gate

Now that you have started your company, you begin to get that nice, comfortable feeling as you realise that, at last, you are your own boss. From now on nobody, but nobody, tells you what to do because it's your business and nobody else's business and, further, it's no business of anybody else how you run it and manage it.

Wrong!

You have probably sensed already that you have to do things that please the customer and that you are acting, to some degree, as their servant or employee. They will certainly tell you what they don't want and it's your job to discover exactly what it is that would satisfy them. We have just spent a few chapters on the subject of satisfying them and emphasising that you can't wait for them to tell you – you have to ask them and understand them.

Otherwise, you can design the perfect company, in your own terms, pull up the drawbridge to defend against the barbarians and have the perfect controlled life that you desire. Your company could be perfectly managed and everything would be hunky dory, except for those annoying barbarians who lack taste and fail to appreciate the good things in life that you offer to them. It begins to feel a bit like ancient Rome, when the barbarian Celts invaded the senate and tugged the senators' beards, just to annoy them.

In the real world you need to know exactly what your customers expect of you. You, in turn, want to know what they are going to give you in return. You also need to know if they have any degree of power that can help or hinder your business and, finally, you need to know what rewards will motivate them to do you some good. In addition to the large tribe of barbarian customers, there are a number of other tribes that have an interest in your business. Suppliers of goods and services to your business are interested in you, as are the members of your distribution chain such as wholesalers and retailers and, of course lenders of money. Other stakeholders have an interest in your business and these might include joint venture partners and shareholders. We will inspect this lot in this chapter, but there are two other tribes that will need looking at – your employees and your competitors, each of which will be examined in other chapters.

Returning to the customers, you need to know what they want from you and you need to know what their expectations are in respect of how you give it to them. Actually, to sell it to them – there's a *quid pro quo* here. What do they bring to my company in the form of resources that are useful to me?

The primary resource that your customers bring to you is sales revenue, in the form of money. So, whilst you are stretching yourself until it hurts in order to please them, try stretching them with your prices, until it is just short of hurting them. Do not become a fairy godmother to your customers – be proud of your prices and keep them as high as you can. Unless, of course, you believe that what you are selling is garbage.

Customers can bring you another helpful resource. They can do your sales promotion for you and they can do it more powerfully than any promotion your company can do on its own. People are likely to dismiss claims made by a company expressing the excellence of their products, prices and service. Customers expect hype and they dismiss it with a simple phrase: "Well, they would say that, wouldn't they?"

However, a potential customer that hears good things about your products, prices or service from one of their family or friends or colleagues will believe what they say about your attributes. Even strangers on a train can influence the buying decisions of others, if it seems to the listener that the stranger is not connected with your company, except as a customer. For a while, I worked with a company that was engaged in guerrilla marketing and, amongst other nefarious practices, they hired ultra cool guys 'n gals to frequent many clubs and bars and to demonstrate that the drink they loudly asked for was *the* drink of the moment.

Be explicit in asking your satisfied customers to recommend your company, especially if you believe that they are opinion-formers or influencers of others who might become your customers. In young companies the temptation is to offer financial inducements to the opinion-former or influencer and, sometimes, it works. I've seen an overt commission structure operating between real estate agents and lawyers, openly declared by the lawyers to the punter, but mostly it just doesn't work effectively. Financial rewards will encourage referees to refer all sorts of people to you, just for the money, and most of these referrals will simply waste your time. It's much better to have referrals from existing, or previous, customers who will be genuinely interested in referring you to others. Information is power and it confers status on the person who is the source of information; most people like to be the person who knows where to get the best buy. Whereas, an offer of money just makes them feel like a pimp.

Whilst customers bring resources to your company, they also have the power to inflict injury on your company. For starters, they can take their business elsewhere and, if the want to be really nasty, they won't even tell you when or why they have forsaken you. If you don't know why, then you can't correct the fault and you may lose more customers.

Customers, like cigarettes, can be seriously bad for your health. They can sue you if you damage them or fail to supply whatever it is that you supply in a proper manner. Or if you sell goods unfit for purpose, carry out services improperly and not in a workmanlike manner and mislead your customers with false claims of performance. You will need to protect your company by building the very high gates of staff training and insurance cover, else the Barbarians will break through and all will be lost.

Political power is also available to your customers in that they can bad-mouth you to others. This is the inverse of the marketing use of opinion-formers and influencers. Sometimes people form political groups, almost like political parties, and demonstrate their political power against large and well-known businesses. However, it is not just the well-known activists that you need to worry about – you can easily be the target of half a dozen vociferous locals.

Rewards for customers can be very motivating, if the reward scheme is well designed. Everybody seeks rewards and modifies their behaviour to gain prizes. What sort of rewards do your customers want from you? Pizza outlets reward behaviour. As you come through the door and are shown to your table, the kids get rewarded immediately (remember that word 'immediately' in relation to rewards) with colouring books or balloons or toys. You, the parents, do not get rewarded at this time because everybody knows that the decision to go to the pizza place was made entirely by your kids. Because they receive immediate and valuable rewards each time they go there they will want to repeat the behaviour that immediately preceded the reward.

When you leave, the adults get rewarded immediately they pay their bill, usually with tooth-breaking hard candy. Adults value the gesture, even if they hate the candy.

If the rewards are always the same, even the kids will get bored and maybe change their allegiance to another food chain. It can be a bit like menu fatigue and the rewards should be varied frequently. Surprise rewards can be very effective, provided that, like the one-armed bandit payouts, they do not come to be expected every time. The loss when they don't get a reward encourages them to try harder next time. Notice how even the most intelligent and sophisticated people become addicted to those elementary computer games like solitaire and minesweeper. If they won every time they would stop playing.

In summary, customers have an important stake in your company in respect of their expectations of your performance. But they also bring you the scarce resources of money and they can engage in quality promotion of your products, referring others to buy from you. They expect rewards from you, even if the reward is only a genuine smile from the person who serves them. Keep in mind that customers can take their business elsewhere and can damage your reputation, if they feel so inclined. If you notice that they have gone, track them down and find out what you did wrong.

If you are selling a product using retailers as the distribution chain you need to determine what they want from you. Their primary interest will focus on their desire for a large gross margin on sales of the product to their customers. The differentiation of your product in the marketplace will be important here, as it allows for higher selling prices and prevents the buyers from making direct comparisons with products from other companies. If you can gain a high retail price from the consumer buyer, then you can afford to offer a higher gross margin to your retailer.

You can reinforce your differentiation advantage, from the retailers' point of view, by giving the retailer some exclusive territory, promising not to approach any of the retailer's rivals. Make known to your retailers a recommended retail price and persuade them not to engage in a price war.

Retailers may need help in displaying your product and you need to understand the point-of-sale materials that will encourage sales, especially the packaging. Consider employing a merchandiser who visits the retailers, ensuring that your product gets the best selling positions and that the point-of-sale materials and the product displays are clean and tidy. If you use dump-bins to encourage sales, make sure that they are not tidy! The merchandiser should also be able to advise the retailers' sales people in respect of the best way to sell the product.

In return for all the stuff you give the retailers, in order to satisfy their expectations, they give you resources that would be difficult or expensive for you to get for yourself. Retailers give you a point-of-sale that end-user buyers recognise as a place to buy your product. If you are an importer of wines, do not try to sell them through builders' merchants – beer may be good, but wine bad. Similarly, if you produce fine table linen you will have difficulty selling through a retailer in a downmarket part of town.

The greatest resource that retailers can give you is prime retail space, free of charge, to get your product in front of the customers. Even if your product doesn't sell much, it costs you virtually nothing. If you happen to be a retailer, try charging your suppliers graded premiums for the best selling spots in your store (don't tell them I said that – please pretend that you thought it up all by yourself). The retailers also provide you with sales people, free of charge, to sell your product. They give you window space, promoting your company and your products to all and sundry. How much would you have to pay in advertising costs to achieve that much publicity?

On the downside, retailers have considerable power over you, due to the quality and quantity of the resources that they make available to you. If they refuse to stock your product, your sales revenue will decrease. They can use your product as a foil against which to sell other products from which they gain a greater gross profit margin. For example: "Madam, we have a choice of three makes – that one is quite good, but I think it's high-priced and not good value. This one is the cheapest, but it tends to fall apart quickly. This one is the best value – reliable, safe and well-priced. Will you take it now or would you like us to deliver?"

Retailers that do not stock your product will happily, if discretely, bad mouth you and your product. Is it criminal slander? No, it's just advice to a customer, a professional opinion, sought and given.

So what rewards can you give to a retailer that will motivate them to sell more of your product? Perhaps 'Retailer of the Year' award, with runners-up, awarded in some exotic location, all expenses paid. Invite retailers that you haven't been able to get your products into so far, as guests – make them envious!

When a product is complicated or expensive, the sales assistant in the retail outlet will be a major influence on the buyer, due to his or her knowledge of the product and alternative products. If you need assistants to push your product, then reward them. Train them in how to sell your product, the training course taking place in another exotic place. Maybe 'Sales Person of the Month', cash, badge, holiday voucher and so on. Remember to thank them within earshot of their colleagues. Motivate them as if they were your own employees which, in a way, they are.

If you have the misfortune of being lumbered with a distribution chain that includes a wholesaler, you have my deepest sympathies. No doubt you have already experienced their complete lack of interest in your product and have realised that you have to be the one to motivate the retailers to buy from the aforesaid wholesaler.

Wholesalers stock many products from many different suppliers and the products that produce the greatest gross profit are the products that they push into the retailers. They may achieve the gross profit by way of high gross margins or by large quantities of sales, or a combination of both. The wholesaler likes products that are trouble-free; they do not like returns from unsatisfied customers. Wholesalers would love you to deliver small, but expensive, products that are properly packaged for the particular market, are easy to store and handle when delivering. As well as wanting high margins from you, they will want you to spend a small fortune on 'pull-through' advertising and promotions, targeted at both the retailers and the end of the line buyer.

So what goodies do they bring to your table? The primary resource that they offer is storage space and stock-holding management. When you manufacture or import, the wholesaler will take in your product in bulk, saving you the cost of a warehouse. They will 'break bulk' and deliver in smaller quantities to suit your retailers, saving you the cost of a fleet of trucks or the cost of using carriers. In theory, at least, they will provide a sales force thereby saving you a large wage bill and all the problems that go with managing a sales force.

What power do wholesalers have over you? Not a lot. If they dump you there is usually another waiting for you round the next corner. If that fails, you can forward integrate, setting up your own wholesale operation. If the thought of running a wholesale operation, with a sales force and a fleet of trucks, makes you feel slightly queasy, wait until the last section of this book when a methodology is revealed that might help you.

What rewards will motivate a wholesaler? If you can get to the sales people who visit or telephone the retailers you might be able to discover what motivates them as individuals. It might be as easy as providing a pair of tickets for a rock concert. The problem is finding out what each sales person has done for you, and you may not be able to discover that information in a timely fashion. A possible solution is to offer free product sales training, during which you can establish relationships with each individual, making it known that you want to reward them personally if they sell your products. It's likely that they will let you have the sales figures, person by person, in order to collect their reward.

A little further out into the world from your company than the wholesaler is the agent. This is a sales person who acts on your behalf and maybe for other companies, too. Typically, they find retail customers, open accounts for your product, take the orders and refer them back to you. You do all the rest – picking, packing, delivering, invoicing, insuring and taking back product returns. You pay the agent a commission on completed sales.

What does an agent expect of you? Nothing is expected but an agreed commission on sales. The resources that they bring to your table are sales of product, opening of new accounts, information relating to the market and the customers' behaviour. Agents are very useful beasts to use in developing a new market, allowing you to evaluate and learn and react before committing large amounts of cash to that market. It is very, very important that you extract all that information from the agent before taking over the operation using your own people. You may have to devise a system that allows you to talk with the customers directly, perhaps a running 'market research survey'. Agents tongues can be loosened by taking them to dinner frequently, when all will be revealed in respect of the relationships formed with the customers. On one occasion I kept our man in Amsterdam up 'til 5 o'clock in the morning in a Brussels hotel – a very productive session. Well, he couldn't really drive back to Amsterdam after all that wine at dinner, could he?

To convert potentially hostile barbarians at the gates of your company you must do what the Romans did and convert them into allies. Our Latin predecessors paid a great deal of attention to the leaders of the tribes, usually making them appear as more majestic to their underlings. That satisfied the leader and the followers fell into line behind their boss. Flattery can get you anything, if you flatter the right person.

If you want a trouble-free business then you have to acknowledge the existence of potential barbarians, anybody that is affected in any way by your existence. More importantly, you have to react to their behaviour initially and, as you become familiar with their behaviour, you can begin to anticipate their needs and wants. Sort of like customers, really.

We have discussed the major tribes of barbarians, but there are many more that you need to consider. They include bankers, lenders, leasing companies, landlords and those from whom you rent stuff. They also include share and stockholders, maybe joint venture partners and suppliers, to you, of goods and services. Even trade organisations should be considered.

When people are starting up in business and they seek advice from various worthy organisations they are almost inevitably told that the first step is to produce a business plan for their bankers. "Why?" asks the would-be entrepreneur. "Because the bank will need to see your plan so that you can borrow money from them" is the worthy reply. My view is somewhat different, in that the vast majority of surviving businesses have not borrowed money in order to start up. They have started their business using only their meagre savings, buying small amounts of product, adding value through their own efforts and reselling for a profit. Their results are the evidence that the business either works or fails. If it works, they grow and make profits which they reinvest in their business. Only then should they borrow to cover stock fluctuations due to seasonality variables. It's even easier now to validate your business idea using internet sites – eBay and others – that allow very cheap mechanisms for testing the market for goods or services.

Would-be entrepreneurs sometimes approach me with the intention of producing a forecast business plan and then funding it by borrowing a lot of dosh from the bank. My reply is to ask them to make a list of half a dozen companies that have been successful by the forecast and funding route. None have managed it so far, and some have simply dropped the idea, whilst others have done a reality check and started to test the market before committing significant cash or planning time to the business.

My objection to borrowing is limited to unproven start-up ventures and my rule is: borrow only the amount that you can lose without causing serious damage to yourself or your business. Always take into account that there might be a 100% failure of your project. Forget probabilities; it is impossible to calculate them accurately in real life new situations and, even if you did, you would have to set up many companies on the basis that one probably will succeed. If you are into taking chances, do the lottery; less downside, more upside. Borrow when your business is proven and do so only to support seasonal variations. Accept that you will grow slowly in the first year or two. Do not attempt to borrow your way out of a loss-making business; if you do, you will go down with the ship.

What resources your banker brings to you, in addition to borrowing facilities, include a very efficient money transaction system, with management records online for many years past. They will also guide you through, and process, foreign exchange transactions and even allow you to hedge your losses against known future payments or receipts in foreign currencies.

Banks can exercise power over you in only one respect: they can withdraw your loan facility. The only reward they will want is interest payments on loans and charges for whatever services that you use. Treat them like any other supplier and shop around for the best deals.

Share and stock holders bring you money as a resource. In the early days of the life of a business the entrepreneur will often seek investment from family and friends, frequently getting small amounts that way. Other business founders will be overcome with their new paternalistic position and feel that they have to provide for their pseudo-children – their employees. So they seek information for share options schemes for their employees. After all, it doesn't cost anything to offer share options, it's not like *real* shares, is it? Not now it isn't. But later, when the company is worth a lot of money, the arguments will start and the frustration will cause the loss of good people and maybe the demise of the company itself.

Another kind of shareholder can be a partner in a joint venture. For instance, if your company were based in Idaho, USA and you wanted to break into the Chinese market, you might (maybe should) consider seeking a Chinese partner. Your joint venture partner will expect that there is a division of shares in the newly formed Chinese company.

What resources will your partner bring to the table? They can bring intimate knowledge of the local customs and practices, in terms of acceptable selling techniques, the hiring of local people, provision of the right sort of premises, possibly distribution facilities and knowledge. They might expect you to bring the product or service technology to the new company.

The partners will typically have a fairly balanced power distribution. Depending on the contents of the contractual arrangement, both partners can unilaterally withdraw from the partnership and go it alone. This happens frequently – there are very few joint ventures that survive in their original state for more than a short number of years. If you teach your partner, then you will probably end up with a competitor in due course. Both parties have the power to withhold information from each other. Both parties will derive rewards in proportion to their contractual agreements in terms of increases in capital value of the company and maybe dividends. They may also consider the information gained from the other as a form of reward. It is wise, therefore, to go into a joint venture as a student, rather than as a teacher, expecting the break up in the not-so-distant future.

Trade associations as stakeholders can bring you resources by listing you as a recognised trader, fit to be a member of this august trade association. One of my clients, an architectural practice, threw themselves wholeheartedly into the trade association for companies with an interest in construction developments. They joined the committees and raised their profile with the developers of sites and the construction companies that carried out the building works. They very soon became a recognised and valued brand in their market segment and grew substantially and profitably.

The rewards expected from you by the trade association are your membership and the fee. The power that they can exert over you is the ability to exclude you from the association.

Two more stakeholders are important to consider – suppliers and competitors, and these are considered in the next chapter. But the most important stakeholders of all are the people that you employ, and they will be covered in the Empowerment Phase section.

Chapter 12

New Kids on the Block

Like any new kid on the block you will want to explore the new territory. You need to find out where all the different facilities are located and how to use them. You will need to know who's who, where you can buy stuff, who's selling what and for how much. Where you now live there are good guys and bad guys, good people to deal with and baddies that are out to get you. New kids know nobody and nobody knows them, which is just as well. You can afford to make mistakes, almost in secret, when you start trading. Don't be in a big hurry to let everybody know that you are now in town until you are reasonably confident that you know who your target customer is and that your product has been adapted to suit that customer. Then you can spread your wings with an awareness campaign.

When you start trading you will need to buy stuff in order to run your company and that might include buying in the raw materials for manufacture or completed products if you are an importer, a wholesaler or a retailer. You will have to find appropriate suppliers and, because you will have only a little money, you will have to try and persuade them to extend credit to you. You have to be careful since, being a new kid on the block, you do not know their reputation. An added complication is that, being a start-up company, you will be husbanding your cash and consequently in search of suppliers that will extend credit to you. The suppliers do not know your reputation either and, without a reputation for honesty, it can be very difficult to obtain credit. To start with you may have to pay cash up front for small quantities, which is very inefficient. But at least you know that, if you persevere, your efficiency will improve very quickly over time.

Where the bad guys come in is when you meet a supplier who will try to take advantage of your lack of experience and, knowing that you will have difficulty getting supplies, will inflate the price as well as demanding cash up front. They also expect you to go bust pretty quickly. After a few months of trading and persistence in approaching suppliers again and again, you will find suppliers gain more confidence in you and gradually contracts between you will change from spot contracts to regular relationship contracts. It's exactly like building a relationship with a new customer, one who is likely to be a regular.

The main resource that suppliers bring to you is 'buy now, pay later' finance, the cheapest form of working capital that you can get. Frequent deliveries help to keep your investment in stocks low, improving your cash flow and allowing you to use less space for stockholding. If you can get the supplier to deliver direct to your customers you cut your costs again and, if you can get your customer to pay up front you are on your way to owning a bank.

When you are established as a business there is a switch of power in your relationship with the supplier. Usually, they need your business more than you need their supplies, assuming that you have a choice of suppliers. You can play one off against another. However, if a supplier that is vital to your business is the only supplier, then they will be able to exert power over you, usually expressed as high prices.

If you are unhappy with the prices or service of your suppliers you could try and 'backward integrate', which means become your own supplier. Sometimes it can be cheaper and more efficient to control the whole process yourself. You can consider this sort of thing when you've read the last section of this book.

Consider also the opposite case, where the supplier 'forward integrates' into your type of business. A real life example of this is the mailing house, Woods & Co, a company that handled mail promotions for many very large companies. The mailing house designed the layouts, kept and maintained the databases, mailed the items but sub-contracted the printing.

The owner of this business had a very capable operations manager who had formed good personal relationships with both the customers and the suppliers. The founder became ill and was unable to work for about three months. During that time his manager left the company and joined the printing company, taking many of the major customers with him. The printer had now forward integrated and was running a full-service mailing house, with in-house printing.

Having just started your company you have no customers and, being the new kid on the block you need to locate them. Whatever it is that they need they are, probably, already being looked after by an existing company and you have a problem. You are going to have to switch the customers from their existing provider to you, and to switch is a bitch.

How do you know who your competitors are? To answer this question you need to define your product in terms what it provides for the customer, and try to define who your customers are – this must be by trial and error in the early stages. Impose a geographical restriction, marking out the territory where you want to promote to and serve your customers. Many service companies in London define their territory as 'inside the M25' – the London equivalent of the Beltway around Washington D.C. Invariably, the service companies happily forget this self-imposed restriction when approached by a nice juicy customer from outside the area – and quite right, too. Your market is for your customers to decide, not for you to decide, thereby chaining yourself by the leg, as in the Indian elephant's training situation. When the chain is removed, the elephant still sticks to its patch. At the time of writing, a client of mine had defined its area of operations as the European Union (psychologically comfortable). But when unsolicited enquiries started to emanate from Russia, Ukraine and Georgia they appointed an Eastern Europe manager to develop that region.

Having had a bash at the definitions (assumptions?) of your marketplace, then ask the customers who they buy from and why. You can safely ignore apparent competitors that are never mentioned by your customer base.

Most of the advice to small companies starts with the exhortation that a business plan must be produced and, more specifically an analysis of the company's strengths and weaknesses and opportunities and threats. Most companies do not realise that 'strong' and 'weak' are comparative terms and have to be compared with something else to validate them. The comparison is, of course, with the competitors' strengths and weaknesses. A fully qualified marketing manager of a central London company that engaged in graphic design listed the following under the heading of 'strengths': "We have Central London offices". There are somewhat more than 100 graphic design companies in central London, all competing for the same customers and all with Central London offices. Having been obliged to comment on hundreds of business plans, my view is that this is typical of virtually all of them.

In order to make a comparison between strengths and weaknesses, in the conventional manner, you would need to define what you were looking for in advance and that is impossible. Even if you think you know what to look for, you will have considerable difficulty in finding anything useful. Some people think that market share is important. A company could say that they have 100% market share – in their street. Wow! Brilliant! Or should we include the next two streets? Or a district of the city? Or the whole city? What about the suburbs and adjacent towns? Region? Country? Continent? The world? What about the universe?

Companies tend to select the geographical area that will show them in a flattering light.

Unless you are comparing your company with a handful of national companies and share is computed by an independent researcher, it is unlikely to be even close to the truth. So, you think that you can establish your share? How do you establish who your competitors are and how do you establish their share? Even if you could establish market shares, in what way will you use them to give you an advantage? Please write your answers on a postcard; or maybe just on the back of a postage stamp.

Here's an example of a weakness within a real company that had been trading for several decades. A serious decline in sales and profits had begun about two years previously and the directors did not know why or what to do about it. Wandering about and quizzing managers and junior staff with open questions I discovered that two years previously an old man, who was employed in the workshop since the inception of the company, had died. His job was to design and customise security alarms to suit the customers' requirements.

When the old man died the directors did not replace him – they couldn't have found another like him, anyway. So from then on the company simply bought in alarms. The alarms were no longer customised to suit the particular application so the customers could buy the same alarms from other distributors. The alarm company had lost its differentiation, which was its major strength. Yet, the people in the company did not know their own strength, a competitive advantage derived from one person, an old man in the workshop. If this company was a competitor of yours how would you have determined this competitive advantage? Bugging the boardroom would have resulted in nothing useful. The answers to the questions that were necessary had to be asked of the junior staff and they provided only piecemeal information that had to be put together to make sense.

The amount of work involved in investigating competitors does not justify that sort of research, when you don't even know what you are looking for until it pops up and hits you on the nose. And why do you need the information, anyway? Business leaders worry far too much about competitors, but they never know what to do about it. For instance, there is a tendency to react to price cuts by a company that is assumed to be a competitor by reducing one's own prices immediately. If a 'competitor' drops their prices, ask your customers about it; do they know it has happened? Maybe not, so why worry about it – let the presumed competitor throw away their profits. If your customers do know about the price-cutting, ask them if they have switched to your competitor. If the switching is slight then do nothing, other than find out why they don't switch away from you.

What prevents them switching? If you want to know anything about your competitors, ask your customers. If they also use other suppliers then interview them thoroughly and find out how you compare, in the view of the customer. It's much more effective than sitting at a desk writing 'We have offices in central London'.

The competitor analysis trap was created by management theorists who discovered that the works of the Chinese military philosopher, Sun Tsu, proposed strategies that could also be applied to the operation of a company. These ideas were immediately popular because, very often, they could be expressed in attractive, memorable one-liners. The European military strategist, Carl von Clauswicz, who wrote on the philosophy and strategies of war, added to the popularity of the 'business is war' analogy.

The art of business is not an act of war. Carl von Clauswicz defined war as the continuation of politics by other means. The art of business is not politics, either. The lack of trust that most people perceive in politicians and the negative campaigning that they engage in are created by the limited spaces available for politicians to gain a seat of power. Their competitors for those seats are usually small in number, perhaps two or three, encouraging investigation of each other in order to eliminate their rivals. In business there are lots of different places to sit and finding yourself a unique seat is much easier than competing for a political appointment.

Business is the art of seduction and the slogan of business should be 'make love, not war'. Give flowers to your customers; washing powder manufacturers did exactly that with plastic daffodils. The customers should be the focus of the managers' attentions. Delight the customers, amuse them, reassure them, comfort them and be firm, but forgiving, if they try to cheat. Most of all, they must trust you to deliver the goods. Then, hopefully, they will fall in love with you.

In my experience, most directors of companies are unsure of how to run a company. Intuitively they realise that there are far too many variables to cope with when making business decisions. In desperation, and perfectly logically, they cast about trying to locate others of their kind, so that they can find out what the others are doing and copy them. It becomes an expression of group-think and is observable whenever and wherever company directors gather together. The reward gained in imitating other companies is the rationalisation that if others are doing it, it must be right. If everybody else is doing it, then it is definitely right. Companies, that are in the same field, all tend to adopt the same strategic approaches, the same tactics, the same processes and management structures.

Strategic groups are an observable feature in various types of business operation.

There are chains of outlets for pizzas, burgers and fried chicken, all adopting the same strategies, worldwide. Perhaps you have noticed that women's fashion clothing and accessories are all alike in the location of their stores, their displays of goods and their 'what's in this season' colours and designs. None of them have to do this, but if they try a more radical approach and fail it will be newsworthy and the adventurous management will ridiculed by the sheep in fashionable clothing. Sometimes, in the academic literature, it is proposed that strategic groups are a product of fundamental economic drivers. It is more likely that fear of the unknown drives companies into herds and fear of ridicule controls the behaviour of their managers and keeps them in herds. Fear of ridicule is a very powerful driver of conformity.

There is an advantage here which, as a newcomer, you can exploit. Strategic groups produce strategic recipes in relation to systems and processes and internal management structures. Consequently, a newcomer, not being familiar with the industry cookbook, is likely to come up with an innovative approach and, without the behavioural controls of a strategic group, the risk of novelty might pay off much better than copycat conformity. After all, a difference that is of value to your customers will allow you to get better prices, leading to bigger profits or faster growth; or both, if kept in balance.

Do not waste time and build false hopes by carrying out an analysis of the strengths and weaknesses compared to your competitors. You will be able to discover all the relevant information from your customers, so long as you build a conversational relationship with a good cross section of customer types. This is a very economical process because the customers will define what they want and what they don't want – exactly the information you need. No chaff to sort from the wheat. No redundant data.

I can find no successful companies that attribute their success to having knowledge of their competitors. Most companies simply ignore the existence of competitors. New entrants to the market are noticed by the existing players if they launch with public promotions, but there is seldom any reaction against the newcomer. There is one very annoying thing that you will discover about competitors. If you appear successful, they will copy the visible parts of your company. If you have a product that can be put in wheelbarrow, they will buy one and attempt to reverse engineer it to discover how it functions and then copy it. With this in mind, make sure that the differentiation that gives you your competitive advantage is invisible to others. Intangible differences, like the old man in the workshop customising alarms, are the most sustainable as they are difficult for others to find and copy. Processes are also difficult for outsiders to define and copy. Consequently, take care of your operating manuals; number and count them in and count them out and remember that, if they are out of your sight they may well be running through a photocopier or scanner. You could lose some differentiation if your processes are copied.

When you start approaching your first prospective customers, find out if they are buying a product from some other company and, if so, find out what benefits they get from that product. Determine what would stop them switching to you. It might substitute be price (don't believe them!), product function or design, service quality or maybe they have signed a three year formal contract with their supplier. If a formal contract, find out when it can be terminated by the customer, so that you can approach them at that time. You might fall foul of the law if you induce them to break their contract; you could be subject to a damages claim against you.

A relational contract, one where the customer and the supplier have a friendly relationship, can be a very strong form of contract and particularly difficult to break. Any offer you make to the customer will be taken back to their friendly supplier, who will be asked to match it and they usually will. Keep this in mind for the time when you will be concentrating on preventing your customers switching away from you. If you trade business to business, then form multi-level relationships between your people and the customer's people. If you form a relationship with only the buyer, then you will lose the relationship when the buyer moves on to another company. But multi-level relationships cause the people to rise up against the new buyer who might try to replace you with his favourite supplier. As the boss, you should form a relationship with the boss of the customer company, wherever possible and your people should form relationships with people at the same level in the customers' company.

In your efforts to gain new customers avoid selling on low prices. The basis of your sales process should be the differentiation advantages that you believe you have over other suppliers, and part of that differentiation might be that you are a better salesperson. Do not sell on price. If you sell on differential advantage you will find out fairly quickly whether or not your advantages are sufficient to enable you to build a business. If not, then you must improve your differentiation and, if you cannot do this then your business will fail quickly.

If you sell on lowest price then you may, as a result, get sales, but you will be stuck forever with a lowest price pitch and your business will drag on and on, profitless, until you run out of cash. A slow bleeding to death of your company is very demoralising and you may not have the motivation, or the cash, to change things and give it another go.

You will need to know how to price your offer, as there is no point in gaining customers unless your company also makes a good gross profit. As a small or medium sized company you cannot cut costs by enough to make any real difference in relation to your competitors. The big players will also have much bigger economies of scale that reduce their unit of sale costs well below yours. Not being able to compete on price, the core of your selling pitch must be based on your differentiation, and you must get the best possible price for each sale that you make.

It is important to know why you price as you do. If you offer a 'discount' you must be quite clear what you are getting for the money that you are giving away. What is the gain to you? If you cannot define the gain, then why give a discounted price?

The demand for sales revenue is put highest on the list by both large and small companies, due to the attraction of size. The question, "What size is your company?" is almost always answered by stating the sales revenue. Accounting convention also puts sales revenue at the top of the profit and loss statement, reinforcing the belief that it is the most important element. You have probably heard the expression 'sales is vanity, profit is sanity' and it is a truism, but mostly ignored by business bosses. Another expression, commonly used is 'the bottom line', meaning net profit, taking its place at the bottom of the profit and loss statement.

Despite these conventions, the most important numbers to achieve are those representing gross profit. That is the difference between your selling price and the direct costs of what you sell. Direct costs include the cost of the product, or materials to make a product, that you sell to your customers. The cost of labour to make up a product is also a direct cost. If you provide a service, for example, maintenance engineers, their cost is a direct cost.

If you chase gross profit and not sales revenue, then you will be driven to sell at the highest price you can get. You will also be driven to reduce your buying-in costs and your direct labour costs, usually the largest cost element in your business. Driving down your direct costs means improving your productivity and your gross profit.

Curiously, in most small and medium sized companies, prices and direct costs take a back seat in the mind of the owner managers and the focus is on sales revenue and overheads. The boss screams blue murder over the cost of telephone calls (1.2% of total expenditure) whilst giving a discount to a favoured customer sufficient to pay the phone bills for a year. The cost of direct labour (maybe 30% of total expenditure) and productivity rates are also overlooked in favour of groaning about the lack of profit on the bottom line. No company has ever been saved by driving down overheads and companies that go bust do so as a result of having silly pricing policies, low gross profit margins and poor productivity rates. There is a mantra in the business world which says you should prepare a 'break-even chart' as part of your start-up preparations. If you do, it will soon be out of date as costs and prices gained will vary as you increase production. Rely on the reality of the management accounts, month by month.

Do not go for growth at the expense of gross profit margins; growth will follow more easily, once your profit margins are right. The very worst policy is to offer high service levels or high quality products and low prices. This is fairly common amongst small companies, which is why they remain small. Such a policy guarantees stagnation in the short term and, in the medium term, complete failure. You cannot offer genuine diamond rings for a dollar each and hope to become rich.

If you have a range of products then you can play with prices; if you have a line that you must sell at a low gross margin, then increase the price of another product to compensate. Do not be rigid in fixing prices overall; use the mix to achieve your margin. How do you know what the right price is? Having first sold it on its benefits, you find out the price by first offering it to buyers at the highest price you dare. If, after a few tries, no one accepts the price, then go back to the buyers quickly and offer a 'special' deal, at a lower price. Try to avoid publishing a price list and change your prices frequently, some going down – special offers – others going up at the same time.

In setting prices try avoid working out the cost price to you and basing your selling price on a given percentage uplift. This is probably the most common and the worst way of setting prices. The right prices are the prices that the market will accept. If you produce bespoke work for each customer then price for each customer. Remember that nobody worries about the price of toilet tissue because it is a small part of their total expenditure. If your offering also represents a small part of your customer's total expenditure, then you can price high.

If an important regular customer is going through a hard time be aware that they need to cut costs and that they will be pressing suppliers, like you, for lower prices. Whilst taking care in advancing credit to a customer in financial trouble, you could make an offer to help them out by giving a time-limited discount. Specify the discount period and stick to it, describing the offer fully in writing and reiterate the offer on each of the invoices you send.

If you have a trusted brand then that alone will enable you to get a better price. There's no need to think that a brand has to be Coca-Cola or MacDonalds; you can be a trusted brand to only one customer. Local traders have a local brand

and if they are trusted to deliver the goods then they will see off any larger predators. Make relationships with your customers and they will pay more for the peace of mind and the caring attitude that you demonstrate to them. Give them a surprise gift every now and then, like the motorbike courier who turns up with a bag of donuts for the people in the public relations firm; when something has to go somewhere fast, who do you think they call first?

Rewarding buyers works and, in large organisations, the best reward is helping them to keep their job. 'Nobody ever got fired for buying IBM' is a well-known phrase meaning that the buyer needs reliability first. Convince them that there is little point in paying a lower price when the result is they lose their job or their reputation because what they buy doesn't work properly. Making a personal friend of the buyer also works well and, if the customer has a high spend, it is worth spending some time on developing the relationship. If a rival company attempts to switch them away, a friendly buyer will let you know and give you a chance to better the rival offer.

If you sell to other businesses and what you are selling is vital to *their*

product offering they will pay more. For instance, if you service kitchen equipment for restaurants, be aware that they cannot produce their product if their cooking appliances are compromised in some way. It's worth big money to be there when they need you. The same principle applies if you are making the braking systems for a customer who sells motor vehicles or aircraft.

Section 4

Processes

Chapter 13

The Money Machine

In the pursuit of the golden fleece of successful company growth you might well adopt the name Jason, but you must change the name of the Argonauts to the Cybernauts. Cybernetics refers to systems that do something and then feed back information in a sort of loop and use that information to modify their behaviour, all to better conform to the desired result. A thermostat on a central heating system operates as a cybernetic system, using the rule: IF the room heat equals 75 degrees F, THEN turn off boiler, ELSE carry on as before. In a business situation the system might be this: IF gross profit is less than last month, THEN check prices and check direct costs, ELSE carry on as before.

Having been in the Reactive Phase for the last couple of years or so, you will find that you are tending to repeat behaviour patterns that produce positive results, whilst dropping patterns of behaviour that result in negative outcomes. This will be happening 'organically' and sometimes without you being conscious of it. You are learning suitable business systems and processes in the same way that you learned to walk or talk or play ball games. There seems to be an innate desire inside many of us, driving us to do things at least as well as others do them. In your case a desire to run a successful business results in learning how to do so over time.

This method of learning takes us back to the process of induction that we encountered earlier in attempting to predict the behaviour of customers. Remember Joe, the regular at the pub and Josephine, the barmaid who learnt his behaviour pattern? "The usual, Joe?" and Joe nods as she is already pouring a pint of his usual beer. But is Joe happy? Probably yes; his nod indicated that all was well. The system is: IF Joe comes into the bar, THEN ask "The usual, Joe?" Wait for feedback nod, then pour beer, ELSE elicit reason for change from Joe OR continue to attend to other customers.

Learning by induction is learning by experience and, like Josephine behind the bar, you have learned a great deal through your experience in the Reactive Phase. The people that you employ will also have learned patterns of behaviour from both customer interaction and from you and your guideline indications of what pleases you. Your people will also be learning how to please themselves, which may not always be to the benefit of you and your company. There will be maybe hundreds of feedback systems created and operating inside you and your people, without conscious effort, with one system for each of the customers' wants and needs. Hang about for a while in a retail outlet and observe the slight changes in the body language and voice tone of the assistants as they interact with different customers. There will also be many systems operating purely for the selfish benefit of your employees and, indeed, yourself. At times, you may know there is a better way to manage the company but, quite naturally, you don't like doing it that way.

If you have a seasonal business you will need to demonstrate different behaviours relating to different seasons, both front-of-house and in the back office. If you are clothing retailer, you will increase your stocks of lightweight clothing in the spring and allow it to decrease in the winter. You may need more employees coming up to Christmas time then you need in August and, if not systematised, you might leave it too late to hire the best people.

As the company grows you will be less able to do everything yourself and there will be quite a few things that employees can do better than you. You will want to ensure that the learning during the Reactive Phase is not lost, either by being forgotten or by some of your people leaving the company. You will not be able to be with your employees all the time, yet you have to ensure that things are done in order to satisfy the customers and make a profit. You also need to control what the economists call 'moral hazard' and what most people call perks, pleasing themselves at the company's expense. Systems will enable you to satisfy the company's requirements with the optimum efficiency. Since 'optimum' is perfection, let's call it 'satisficing' – satisfying to the level of being acceptably sufficient. If you fail to formalise the company systems by casting them in stone – limestone rather than granite, as they will need to be carved a bit as time goes on – your company will stall, you will not be able to grow further and you will never make any money.

You cannot afford to run out of Joe's favourite beer; if you do, you will lose him as a customer. You must devise a stock control system that works by feeding back information on stock levels of all of your products to the buyer who replenishes the stock. The buyer may not be human if the system is purely for replenishment, just a few lines of code in a program will do the job. There are many computerised stock control systems that will allow you to quantify the rate of sale of the product, its lead time from order to delivery, and the maximum level of stock you can afford to hold.

Accountants will tell you not to overstock as it will absorb too much of your working capital and the cost of money is the return you could get on it elsewhere. However, my emphasis would be that you should never, ever run out of Joe's beer, because the cost of losing a regular customer will dwarf the interest cost and other costs of holding stock. One of the reasons the big supermarkets are putting the local retailer out of business is that the big boys know their regulars through loyalty cards swiped at the till, know what they want to buy and how often they do so. Then they tailor their systems to suit the needs of their customers. It is not rocket science, its more like Lego – anybody can do it if they really care about their customers sufficiently to buy and operate these systems properly for the benefit of your customers and your business.

From the moment that you start trading you should be running a computerised accounting system, with someone responsible for accurately inputting the data and someone competent enough to produce accurate management accounts. A computerised system imposes a discipline which manual systems lack; manual systems allow for all sorts of errors to remain undetected. You need to know, right from the start, that you are making a gross profit and which products or services are contributing the most money to your coffers.

Even if, at the beginning, you operate a perfect customer service, you can be losing a lot of money whilst doing so. You will not please your customer for long when you begin to run out of stock due to running out of cash. The customer won't care much when, shortly afterwards, you put the shutters up and go home. That is, you can go home if you haven't already mortgaged you house to the bank in order to finance the business. The numbers relating to performance must not be neglected, in the early stages of a business, especially the gross profit level.

A firm of electricians used to work out their price per hour by first working out what their cost per hour was for the electricians. The electricians were paid for a 37 hour week, with additional payment for working overtime. The firm worked out the cost of a 37 hour week and the electricians' average travel costs for a week and divided it by 37. They fed the resulting cost figure into their computerised costing and pricing system. Then they added a fixed percentage mark-up to the cost to produce the price that they charged the customer. The prices were the same for all customers, all types of jobs and for all electricians.

When the job was completed they examined the cost sheet and congratulated themselves on the completion of another profitable job. However, the management accounts each month showed that the gross profit for the company was always about 25%, whereas the gross profit on the costing sheets indicated about 40%. The company struggled on, barely surviving, for many years. You may have guessed the reasons for the difference. Electricians may be paid for 37 hours per week but do not work for 37 hours every week. Holidays and other absences, non-chargeable 'go-backs' on badly done jobs, non-chargeable housekeeping paperwork, care of vans, replenishment of van stocks, malingering and so on all reduce the chargeable hours significantly. Different electricians were paid different rates, according to their seniority. Over time the problem got worse because the company did not update the costing figures very often.

When something that you do produces a desired result, there is a very reasonable tendency to continue to do the same thing. The achievement of a desired result is a reward and consequently motivates you to repeat the behaviour. When you repeat the behaviour you expect the same result, as when you get into your car and switch on the ignition you expect the engine to operate properly, as usual. If, at some point, your behaviour does not elicit the expected reward, there is a natural tendency to attribute the failure to a one-off exception to the rule and to continue to do the same thing. The longer the system being used has been successful, the more likely it is that the operator continues to use the same behaviour and persists with the system. They will carry on, despite mounting evidence that the system is past its sell-by date.

This is where the Cybernauts come in. The Cybernauts are the people who design or select the systems that keep your business not only functioning, but performing to a satisficing level. Cybernauts look after the systems, modifying them as necessary and ensuring that they are always up to date. Who or what are these creatures, these products of *Blade Runner*?

The Cybernaut responsible for the functioning of the accounting system might be your in-house accountant. He or she can design a high-level system to allocate responsibility for each of the systems to one person, including the timescales that show when the systems are to be regularly reviewed.

Your lawyer is a Cybernaut and you might decide that she appears every year in the month of March and audits, from a legal standpoint all your legal obligations including sales contracts, employee contracts and so on. She is also taxed to improve the systems where necessary and generate improvements resulting in greater efficiency.

Similarly, your computer and information Cybernaut might be an external consultant or adviser. If they work with many different companies they are more likely to know what's currently happening as far as systems are concerned. Your marketing systems should also be overseen by both an external expert conducting, say, an annual audit to uncover faults and make suggestions relating to new developments that might improve the systems. As you grow, an in-house Cybernaut might be you, as the boss, or a marketing manager. If you employ a marketing manager, make sure you continue direct contact with customers; as the boss, you need to know and you need to question systems, taking care not to de-motivate the Cybernauts. Asking questions is more motivating than telling them what to do.

A simple example of an external adviser comes from the finance director of a company who, once a year, will have a meeting with a specialist tax accountant, to help formulate the tax policy for the company for the coming year. It is far too inefficient for the finance director to keep up with the changes in the tax regime and to understand them to the extent that they can be exploited to best advantage. The specialist will have all that knowledge in his head and can quickly help the finance director to change the company systems in respect of taxation.

One of the jobs of a Cybernaut is to regard a single failure of a system as a signal that the system might need modifying or changing more radically. Change disturbs people and the process of change is inefficient and costly. Don't make changes to systems immediately unless it is obvious that it needs changing immediately or could be changed without causing disruption. The Cybernauts should record the failure, discuss it with the system operator and seek a solution. Frequently, it is better to wait until there are a few more improvements before making a more holistic change to the system. Bear in mind that incremental changes are less disruptive than major changes.

Remembering Dr. Flux from earlier chapters, he is always working at changing the environment in which you and your company exist. Even dull old accounting has changed a lot since the Merchants of Venice invented double entry book-keeping several hundred years ago. Little changes are going on all the time and eventually tinkering with repairs no longer works; the system may have to completely change in order for the company to continue to operate effectively. When typewriters changed into computerised word-processors the new systems were easily, and gladly, adopted in the business world.

But major changes can happen suddenly. Business earthquakes do happen and the requirements for system changes sometimes cannot be anticipated and all you can do is to react to them, with an eye on opportunities that might arise from the change, ones that you can exploit. The disaster of 9/11 in New York terminated UK – USA deals for two of my clients in London, both requiring a major adjustment to the overall strategies of the companies. This effect was felt by many, many companies throughout the world. You have often seen the remonstration on adverts for equity funds: 'Past performance is not a guide to future performance'. Henry Ford put it more succinctly: 'All history is bunk'. Bear in mind that all our experience is bunk and only the desperate search for causality that is inherent in humans makes us believe experience is a guide to future performance. If it was so then the business world would be littered with serial entrepreneurs. So where are they hiding? Out of the millions of business owners surely a few thousand could be identified?

Remember the stage hands that move the scenery and show you worlds that exist outside of your mind? Cybernauts are sort of like that, often coming in from outside and showing you new ways to manage your world. External Cybernauts should be balanced by internal Cybernauts so that fast systemic changes can be made when necessary, but fundamental new system developments usually come from outside the company.

When you are monitoring information fed back from your systems, be aware of the effect frequency of information has on your perception of that information. Weird or what? When monitoring information feedback do so by using a longish timescale. The moving annual total, based on monthly data, will provide a trend line which will itself give you information that is relevant to running a business, provided you have been operating for more than a year. Expressed as a graph it can give you early indications of changes in trends and possibly guides to where you are going in the future.

If you measure your performance on a monthly basis, looking at each month's performance on its own or comparing it with different months in the same year, and you believe that information is the truth, the whole truth and nothing but the truth, then you will say, frequently, 'So help me God'. But if you enter data to a moving annual total graph you will observe a truer picture of your performance. List the last 12 months performance, say January to December, and mark the total on a graph. When the next January figures are available add to the total and deduct the previous January's total. Continue with February and so on forever. You will spot trends early that you will miss without a graph.

The rule is: the shorter the time periods that you are measuring, the greater the volatility displayed, producing extreme swings from good to bad. But daily, weekly, monthly movements do not represent your results for the year, an arbitrary timescale in itself. Why not a two year measurement, if it better suits your business? High frequency data on business performance translates into very poor information. You will save yourself the daily dose of tranquilisers if you concentrate on the longer term results rather than the shorter time intervals.

In real life, working with a national service engineer company I observed this phenomenon with all its drama. Perhaps it prevents entrepreneurial bosses from getting bored. The company employed a bookkeeper who also acted as an in-house accountant and who produced the monthly management accounts. The bookkeeper did not understand accruals and prepayments so, when the quarterly rent bill came in it was charged, in its entirety, to the month in which it arrived, instead of being allocated evenly over three months. This ensured that the boss was guaranteed a heart flutter every three months when the accounts revealed that no profit had been made. The following month, with apparently no rent to pay, a bottle of champagne was opened to celebrate the return to profitability.

A further complication was that the direct labour, the largest element of the company's costs, was monitored by weekly time sheets. Instead of allocating the cost of labour by days, the accountant found it easier to have a four week month and sometimes to have a five week month, allocating costs accordingly. When the five week month coincided with the quarterly rent month, the boss firstly panicked and then spent the rest of the month thinking the company was on its way out. Even worse, he made major decisions based on his perception of the company's performance for the month, including firing a senior manager on one occasion.

A larger company, a national high street clothing retailer, measured their sales revenue on a daily basis, as had been done since their foundation in the 1930s. A rainy Monday turned the entire management team into a pit full of hissing snakes for the remainder of the week. Until Saturday, when the till takings inevitably outperformed all the weekdays, as usual. In clothing retail, management has very little power to change things once the buying is completed for the season.

Many businesses are subject to seasonal influences which makes daily, weekly, monthly and quarterly reporting almost useless. In these cases, the moving annual total is all that matters in interpreting the information.

In a wonderful and completely contrary event, one company I worked with had a very confident boss, fearless in his attitude to normal codes of behaviour. He had absolutely no time for accounting data. When the company moved offices, to accommodate increased growth he fired all the accounts employees and threw all the accounting records into a builder's skip. He outsourced the entire accounting function to external accountants. Their brief was simple: keep the company within the law in respect of annual returns and company secretarial legal filing requirements.

A few years later this company became the largest of its kind in the world, not because there was no management accounting, but its growth certainly wasn't compromised by the lack of monthly numbers. It kept performing because the operating systems were well developed and very predictable and there were no major environmental changes that affected the company in any way. Sales figures and head counts of employees were all that mattered as the pricing system was market driven and stable, automatically adjusting itself over time.

Another example sheds some light on marketing systems. A firm of bakers started up with one small corner store, with the bakery out back. Within about 15 months they had opened a second operation – another retail store, with the bakery in the basement. Profits were astonishingly high and the third operation was up and running within another 18 months. We are now talking of a multi-million pound operation with about 70 employees. The interesting aspect was that the directors were completely dismissive of all marketing stuff and would not entertain any advice relating to this 'pseudo-science'.

In reality, there was the most effective marketing operation in place. There was only one tiny office above one of the shops with, literally, only space for one seated person. None of the directors or senior managers had offices and when they needed to write something down they used the nearest shelf or somebody's back as a desk. All the directors and managers frequently served customers in the stores and worked in the bakeries so that there was no need for any marketing information systems. The top guys were receiving the feedback directly from the customers, who were queuing for the cakes and breads. They got immediate response to new products, preferences of different types of customers and the contexts of usage. For instance, they produced specialised packaging for items that were eaten by office workers at their desks. The company charged very high prices and the feedback from customers was that they didn't care about price.

When interpreting profit or sales performance or, for that matter, any other sort of performance, keep in mind the phenomenon of regression to the norm. Here's an example from everyday health checks: errors in taking blood pressure are widespread and failure to allow for regression to the norm often leads to premature treatment. In other words, if you have your blood pressure checked today, it might be very high and treatment recommended. If you have your blood pressure checked tomorrow it could be very low, but will probably be a little lower. The moving annual total graph that we referred to earlier is a system for measuring closer to the norm than being misled by the variations around the norm. If you check your blood pressure at monthly intervals and record the results on a moving annual total graph you will get much safer information and you will be able to pick up on the beginning of a gentle rise that might need treatment.

Generally, if no action that drives performance is taken, then performance tends toward the average. A good performance tends to be followed by a lower, more towards the average, performance. Conversely, a poor performance will probably be followed by a better performance, tending to the average. Very often runs of good performance are attributed to the skill of a particular person when, in fact, it is just a run of luck. Keep your eye on the performance and you will find that it dips back towards the average, the normal performance. It depends on the period over which you make the measurements. It is a bit like that logical teaser: how long is the coastline of the United States? It depends on the size of the ruler. A small ruler will measure more inlets than a large ruler, which doesn't fit into small inlets and consequently yields a greater length for the coastline.

A classic recurrent example is the decline and recovery of major companies. As the company declines, the Chief Executive is blamed and replaced by another CEO. This one apparently stabilises the company, but fails to make any significant improvement. He gets replaced by a third CEO who is hailed as a guru for vastly improving the fortunes of the company and its shareholders. The whole affair is most likely just luck, deriving from the performance moving randomly about the norm.

Keep in mind that this phenomenon is a 'natural' deviation and a special event, like the Twin Towers on 9/11, can alter the pattern. Likewise, if you interfere by changing the procedures and behaviours and the environment in relation to your company you can influence the pattern. If you can apply knowledge as to the causes of performance improvement, then you really can affect the outcome for the better.

If you do nothing extra or different to affect performance then, like a great many smaller companies, you will crawl along consoling yourself that at least you are doing as well as inflation.

Chapter 14

Rerum Novarum Cupidus

In the human body, many ailments are cured by the normal bodily processes of self-preservation, with or without the intervention of a physician or the administration of a treatment. Many ailments appear to be cured by taking some form of medicine, but the truth is that many drugs do not work for a high proportion of the patients who take them. However, if the taking of the drug precedes the recovery from the ailment then it is assumed that the cause is the prescribed medication. We are unaware of the bodily processes that cure the body of its ailments, and this lack of awareness strengthens our belief in the prescribed medicine. For example, many people still ask their doctor to prescribe antibiotics in order to cure their common cold. But the common cold is caused by a virus, not bacteria, and antibiotics have no remedial effect whatsoever. Yet this illusion persists, indicating that the patients have attributed their recovery from the common cold to the dosage of antibiotics.

If we apply the analogy to a company we might find that the introduction of a marketing plan precedes a rise in sales revenues or profits. We attribute the revenue or profit success to the effectiveness of the marketing plan and award a laurel wreath to the marketing manager to wear upon his head.

However, if you work at a lower level than the marketing manager then you may well ignore parts of the plan because you are motivated by your bonus, which is based on the level of sales revenue. Without announcing the fact in public, you simply develop your own workarounds so that you can achieve a higher bonus. At your level in the organisation you are closer to the customers and have a better understanding of their buying motivations. Intuitively, you understand them and react appropriately to their needs and behaviours. What you do is far better than the stuff in the marketing plan. Since they don't really know what you are doing, the management attribute the wrong cause to the increase in sales revenue.

Take care, therefore, to ensure that the processes to be bedded down are the real cause of the success. How do you do that? You involve the people who are most involved on a daily basis in the operation of the system. Take your guidance from the minions, not the managers, and design the system to allow them to do their work well. Fortunately, virtually all employees respond to being valued in the context of their job and will own it and look after it like a pet. A little attention yields a lot of motivation.

If you set out a strict plan, which is a system or process description, with all the behaviours carefully plotted and you set it in motion, you will appear to be doing whatever it is that you planned to do. Unfortunately, you will not necessarily end up in a place that you will like. The marketing steps that you plan to take may seem the best when you plan them, but as you cannot know the future they might not yield the benefits you thought they would.

Many times, in many companies I have seen marketing plans carried out with exemplary dedication, all according to the plan and the result ending up in a major disappointment. In one extreme case a light engineering company employed an external marketing consultant to develop a marketing system with the aim of increasing sales revenue, which had stagnated over the previous couple of years. The company's products were replacement parts for specific types of machines. The consultant worked over a two year period and at the finish sales revenue had dropped by 8% in real terms. The fundamental reason for this failure was that the consultant had not consulted with the customers. The proximate reason was that all the customers were perfectly happy with the products, but obsolescence of the original machines had reduced their need for the spare parts. That information could have been discovered two years before and the approach should have been the development of new products or new markets.

In another dreadful case a retail company achieved its plan of opening several outlets in a new region. From the start, all the outlets were losing money and continued to do so, causing considerable losses. Again, the reason was not engaging with the prospective customers and thereby discovering that regional differences existed in customer behaviour and preferences. The products were wrong for the new region and so were the prices. The company came within an ace of being liquidated and needed a turnaround specialist to put it right.

An important lesson to be learnt was that systems that work well in one context may not work well in a different context, for example in different cultures, different age groups or different sexes. Accepting that the actions that you plan to carry out will be carefully enacted, make sure that the systems you fix into place have been proven in practice. Alternatively, go very slowly and carefully, investing very little in order to survive the worst downside. Test new marketing ideas, inexpensively, and talk to the customers in the target market whilst testing. Scrap the idea quickly if it isn't working.

When you have a run of luck, perhaps resulting in two or three years of rising performance, be careful in attributing it to your vast skill and knowledge. Stay grounded, otherwise your over-confidence will encourage you to take a risk that wrecks the company. In a complex body like a company, the cause of an effect is quite difficult to determine. Distinguish between 'chance' and 'luck'. Each lottery ticket purchased is a chance, but winning is luck. However, the more tickets you buy, the more chances you have of winning. Just make sure that lottery tickets are cheap enough for you to lose your money without doing too much damage to yourself.

Beware of budgets because they have a tendency to transmogrify into targets. Targets, of course, have to be achieved, or else… A sure-fire way to achieve your targets is to reduce them in stature, a technique demonstrated by single-person owned companies, which are a bit scared of growing too big to personally control.

I came across a company trading as a multiple retailer and noted that they were using their budgets as targets. The target for net profit for the coming year was £100,000. After nosing about for a bit, I discovered that the net profit target five years ago was also £100,000. Yet, the budgets were prepared every year, with the boss taking the most interest in the creation of the numbers. It was very pleasing to see the top man in a company achieve his profit targets, year after year. We could do with more like him. In fact, across the expanse of the business world we have many more like him.

Another U.K. company, engaged in the design, manufacture and distribution of metal products, sets out its sales targets every year in its budgets but, recognising that they have no ability to forecast the future, they simply add 10% to last year's actual performance. In the last five years they never hit target; not even once. However, here's the interesting bit.

The managing director of the company met a man from the USA in Germany, at a trade fair. On impulse, they decided to invade the USA and set up Bloggs LLC, registered in Idaho – tax advantages y'know – and started trading immediately, using outsourced logistics and sales force. Within two years and a bit, the sales revenue in the USA was nearly 80% that of the UK company, which had been trading for over ten years. The fact that there was no budget or budgetary control in the American company released them from the straitjacket of targets and they just went for it. With no budgets to act as psychological seat belts, the risks appeared greater and resulted in more effort being made to gain revenue. They didn't know when to stop!

Here's another interesting real-life example to illustrate the perversities of setting sales revenue targets. The marketing manager was also the manager of the sales force and both he and the members of the sales force were rewarded with a bonus on achieving target. The interesting point is that the marketing manager was also the person who decided on the prices. Inevitably, the team hit their sales targets but completely destroyed the profitability due to offering discounts to achieve sales.

In many companies sales people cheat in order to achieve their targets. Having achieved their target for the year, they do not enter any more sales in the books for that year, transferring the sales records into the next year. The reverse of this practice is also used, pulling back orders and deliveries from the next year into the current year in order to achieve target. The extreme is when an order and delivery is completely faked, entered in the current year, the entry being 'cancelled by the customer' in the following year.

Here's a quote from *The Times* (London), dated December 24, 2007): "Targets intended to cut long waits in hospital A & E units have cost the National Health Service £2 billion over the past five years...The extra costs have come from patients who are in danger of having to wait more than four hours in A & E – the target limit – and are admitted to hospital 'just in case'. Many are discharged the same day... Primary Care Trusts have to pay [the hospital] as much as £1,000 per admission. Over the past five years about two million extra patients were admitted to hospital. But in Scotland and Northern Ireland, which do not have the four hour target, there has been no increase in admissions."

Imposing targets on people and punishing them if they fail to achieve the targets invites them to devise workarounds. Like budgets, the feedback comes only when it is negative – 'you have overspent your budget' is a common accusation in the workplace. But nobody ever hears 'you have under-spent your budget, so here is a reward'.

A company is holistic and a target for one element of performance will affect other areas of performance, producing unintended consequences. For example, targeting of sales revenue by individual sales people might result in biased distribution of sales leads by the sales administrator who might be 'incentivised' by a particular sales person.

"When a measure becomes a target it ceases to be a good measure" so says Charles Goodhart, once upon a time the Chief Adviser to the Bank of England, the UK equivalent of the Federal Reserve. Targets distort behaviour and turn decent folk into quasi criminals, not just in business, but in government organisations too.

Create 'budgets' in a different way. Enter up last year's performance on a spreadsheet and project the performance for the year ahead, using the same figures. As the actual performance figures become available each month substitute the actual figures in place of the projected figures. This will disclose the information that, if you continue to perform like this, then the 'projected' result will be whatever the spreadsheet shows at the end of the projected period. If you are not satisfied with the projected outcome, react by doing something different.

As the boss, you have to become the driver. Train yourself to become greedy, dissatisfied by mediocre performance; kick ass if the performance results in less than you want. Reward your people based on actual overall performance, not on individual targets. If you are satisfied with what you are getting, that's all you will ever get – and all your loyal people will ever get – and a major negative event outside your control, is more likely to send you back to the beginning. Not many people can run a successful company; you owe it to others to drive it on and create the wealth.

If you want to judge your own performance, then don't be the only lawyer at your trial. The evidence that you personally put forward will suit your objective of hearing good news, but there will be no objectivity in your supporting arguments. You need a large dose of objectivity and that can only obtained from others. You need a jury that is independent and the best jury you can have is the customers. They can also decide on your punishment, which they can deliver by walking away from your company. They can vote with their feet – "Guilty, Your Honor" – if you fail to provide them with the opportunity of voting vocally.

Reel in the stage hands, those who are familiar with other scenarios, and get them to pronounce judgement, in comparative terms, compared to the performance of other companies.

Our wise adviser to the Bank of England, Professor Goodhart said, "What's counted, counts". Turned around, that says that if you don't count it then it doesn't matter and you can safely ignore it. That is why many companies fail in terms of relating to their customers, whilst producing management accounts diligently every month. If you want your customers to count you must count them and their behaviour, their wants, their needs and the things about your company that bug them.

The management accounts should be accompanied by, not a 'marketing' report, but by a customer report. It should include, for example a heading: 'What did the customers say about us last month?' Include quoted comments such as compliments, brickbats, things they like, things that bugged them and their suggestions and thoughts about existing products and new product ideas. Include who they like to deal with and who they want to escape from, which they might do by switching to another company.

In the customer report you will also want to see their measured behaviour. Produce a head count of active customers this month and apply it to a Moving Annual Total (MAT) in order to expose the annual trend in acquisition and retention of customers. Count the growth in the average spent by each customer, in total and per transaction; plot the trend. Calculate the gross profit from each customer, plot it on the graph and calculate what we would lose over the next five years if we lost that customer now.

Why do we need systems, anyway? Everything that you do for the first time is done with imperfections and sometimes total failure. Our attempts get better and more successful the more we repeat the attempt. These initial failures are so common that we have a widely accepted name to describe the phenomenon: 'teething problems'. These teething imperfections do not please the customers and will figure on their list of dental problems. And we may lose the customer. The dentistry we have to carry out is the extraction of the bad bits and the filling of the cavities until we arrive at a state that is as close to perfection as possible. We want to see the gleaming smiles of our customers.

To make money in your company you need to reduce the original imperfect delivery to a repeatable and perfect production or delivery. As you solve the problems you will reduce the time it takes to produce, and probably the cost of the materials used, to deliver perfection to the customer. You do not have to reduce your prices simply because you are now more efficient, and you may well be able to increase them. Because the systems are repetitive the cost of training your people will be reduced, adding a bit more to your profits. You will also reduce the stress previously experienced by both the customers and your own people. Many people do not want taxing jobs, wanting just to come to work, do their jobs properly and then go home. They might enjoy the company of their fellow workers, but many get their kicks outside of work. If they want real adventure in their workplace they will do what you have done – start their own companies.

The repetitive quality delivery can also be known by another name – consistency. When someone buys a can of Coca Cola they do not criticise it for being exactly the same as the can they bought yesterday; in fact, they welcome it and would complain if it was different. Consistency of delivery is possibly the most important and valuable element of a positive brand. The best known brands in the world are the brands that can repeat the product exactly, time after time, and that's why they are the best known. The customers will complain if the delivery varies, because they effectively own the brand and the company must ask for the customers' permission if they want to change any aspect of it.

You have probably noticed that most people are irrational most of the time; very few people really work out by logic what they are going to do next. They generally stick to the familiar patterns of behaviour in order to feel safe. People are perfectly rational when engaged in a repetitive task, such as driving or brushing their teeth, because the system is rational. Many cooks produce a very desirable meal by using repetitive recipes, but they had to practice actually doing it before they got it right. Someone who seldom cooks will make a pig's ear out of a T-bone steak.

Managing in a company means that novel problems and opportunities arise from time to time and managers will make irrational decisions. To get over the problems of irrationality and inconsistency, found naturally in all people, we design and implement repetitive systems that are rational and consistently produce the desired result. Computer systems and accounting systems are examples of lock-down systems where the operator cannot change the process. As the world changes even these systems tend to drift towards irrationality, hence the need for frequent check-ups to ensure that they continue to produce the desired result and do not produce any unintended consequences. The more repetitive systems you have in place, the more time managers have for reacting to novel events.

You may have noticed that companies have cultures that have grown all by themselves, the result of nobody's intention. These cultures develop myths and legends, rituals, hierarchies and sub-groups. The cultures develop in order to allow repetitive, and therefore predictable, behaviours to form. Just like good manners, everybody knows what to do to avoid upsetting each other. Predictable, unthinking behaviour creates a comfort zone, a stress buster, for the people who work in the company. A stressful company would display its difficulties to the customer base through the normal interactions and would not succeed. It might stay small and nasty, or it might simply fail and go bust.

Where we do not want repetitive behaviours, at least some of the time, is within the Cybernauts, although they may display repetition during their day jobs. When a Cybernaut has created or improved a system and it works well, they will attempt to apply the same solution the next time they meet a problem that is only somewhat similar to the first one. It's a natural behavioural process. If you ran away from the tiger faster than your colleague did and he is no longer with us, then you might run away when you encounter anything that looks like a tiger at first glance. The only way to avoid this natural cul-de-sac is to ensure that more than one mind is applied to the development of systems. Encourage the Cybernauts to discuss problems and solutions in a group; not brainstorming, just changing the scenario by the expression of different views on the solution. One Cybernaut only must carry the responsibility for the system and the outcomes it produces. Beware of those that propound 'best practice' – they are fundamentally wrong, as 'best practice' may be out of date or misapplied to the wrong problem or opportunity.

Involve the employees in the creation of new systems or changes to existing systems. Let them know who the responsible Cybernaut is and allow them access so that they can contribute their ideas to exactly the right person. The involvement of the people who have to operate the systems is vital. They will possess knowledge, frequently tacit and inexpressible, that is vital in the creation of a perfect system. So take their feelings into account and do not rely on logical arguments to the exclusion of intuition. Avoid the future complaints of "It's not my fault – it's the stupid techies". They didn't allow for…" Try leaving your ego on the night table when you go to work and try asking the front line people to define the problem or opportunity and to come up with the solutions.

Resist the temptation to constantly seek change. Cicero quotes Julius Caesar's comments on one of his generals, who was constantly reorganising his troops and his battle plans, as suffering "rerum novarum cupidus" – the lust for new things. It was not meant to be a compliment. Change is inherently costly and should not be engaged in as a sort of hobby. Neither is it necessary unless it is wanted by the customer, in the first place and that it adds to the wealth of the company in the second place. Avoid expressions like 'change management' and do not appoint a change manager who will demand change only to prevent his own redundancy.

Finally, the most important rule of all when creating systems: Test, test and test again whilst you are developing a system or modifying an existing system. Acknowledge that systems are holistic and a change in one part may often lead to unintended consequences in another part. IF you go live with an untested system THEN it will fail publicly ELSE it will cause people to devise workarounds. It might even cause the company to lose customers.

Section 5

Empowerment

Chapter 15

Empowerment (or Delegation?)

In the world of business, 'cooperative' companies are sometimes created, based on the principle that, if all members have equal votes in the company they will be more motivated in their work. This is probably the ultimate in empowering the employees of a company. The initial expectation by the creators of the cooperative company is that having eliminated autocratic, capitalist bosses they will have eliminated exploitation of the workers.

In the early years of being a business adviser I engaged with a few of these cooperatives and found that, with few exceptions, they failed fairly quickly, for a number of reasons. Squabbling between the shareholders was a common and distracting feature of the companies. Contrary to expectations, bosses arose spontaneously, promoted by the power of their personality or their greater intelligence compared to the other members. Bullying and exploitation had not been eliminated and the cooperation assumed by the name was very often absent. The less aggressive and less intelligent members, far from being motivated, displayed the opposite behaviour patterns, arriving late for work and taking little interest in anything to do with the company, including customers. They had a vote, but no real say in anything of importance. Altruistic motivations in the cooperative company do not seem to work very well.

My conclusion was that the concept of 'empowerment' applied to profit making companies does not work very well, and evidence of its effectiveness seems to be absent from the academic research. The only 'evidence' put forward to support the use of empowerment, as a policy, seems to be that, in attempting to implement some not quite understood changes involving the employees, they turned out to be happier. The Hawthorne experiments in the 1930s created increased happiness and increased productivity regardless of the nature of their interventions. Turn the lights up and productivity increases. Turn them down again and there is no decrease in productivity. Any intervention involving employees will improve their happiness because, in most of the larger organisations, they are usually ignored.

As an owner or manager you cannot empower any employee, otherwise you will create a form of anarchy, where people will decide for themselves what they will do and when they will do it. If they chose to ignore the repetitious systems that create the efficiency that produces profits, then the company will fail. What you can do is enable people but not empower them; empowerment is something they do for themselves. You can, and should, give them the training and the skills to enable them to do their jobs without too much effort. You can train them further so that they can acquire skills and learning that will enable them to gain more power through promotion, if that is what they want.

As you grow your company you will need to employ more people and as you do you will find that jobs become more specialised, and consequently the company becomes more efficient. You will also find that the increase in numbers results in too wide a span of control and that you, the boss, can no longer find the time to engage with people as closely as you used to do. Whilst you can be the boss to about a dozen people quite comfortably, as you grow in numbers you will need to create a hierarchical management structure.

In empowerment theory, the fact that you cannot control, say, twenty people or supervise them in any meaningful way should empower them and make them more creative and contribute more to the success of the company. In practise, the opposite happens. What the economists call 'moral hazard' has a field day and grows like a weed. The same phenomenon that appeared in cooperative companies rises from its vampire's coffin and sucks the lifeblood of the company. Increases in poor timekeeping, absenteeism, fiddling expenses, leaving early, stealing the company's property, all become part of the company culture. Nobody gets murdered, but customers get neglected and performance of the company tends towards losses.

Where you get engineers that travel to customers' premises – electricians, plumbers and service engineers of all sorts – the risk of moral hazard is very high. Likewise, in widespread retail outlets, especially when the boss is reluctant to visit the outlying outlets. When this moral hazard is apparent, then there is only one person with the power to prevent it and that is you, the boss. To start with, you ought to get out more. If growth is an objective, there is only one way to achieve it. You will have to delegate to others and you might well be apprehensive about such a step – most bosses are when the Empowerment Phase arrives; but it must be done, if you are to become rich. From now on I shall ignore the word 'empowerment', convenient though its initial letter is in forming the mnemonic 'Carpe Diem', and use the word 'delegation' in its place.

There is a self-help book in the stores called 'Feel the Fear, Then Do It'. Most people feel fear when venturing into the unknown and delegation is an 'unknown' to most entrepreneurs. Delegation is also sometimes resisted by the boss because most of his knowledge is in tacit form and he doesn't know what he knows and doesn't know how to transfer it to a delegate.

When people talk about having a flat organisation they are not thinking in terms of a two-level company, one with the simple structure of the boss and the workers. They are usually referring to an eight or ten level bureaucratic organisation and thinking that it should be reduced to six or seven levels. Delegation is an essential step forward in the growth of the company, and it is also the most psychologically difficult step. But it has to be done; otherwise the company will stay in the same place, going round and round in ever-decreasing circles, until finally it disappears ...

When delegating for the first time, bring in somebody from outside your company to help you define what you want from a new manager, why you want them, what you want them to do and what you expect to be the positive results of promoting or hiring them. Another boss of another company who has already engaged in delegation might be the ideal person to advise you. They will feel pleased that you asked them to help – most people like to feel they are an expert in some field or other.

It is wise to plan ahead for the time that you will reach the Delegation Phase. Start to consider building a management team soon after the Reactive Phase has settled down (but still inviting appropriate reaction as necessary). It can work well if the Processes Phase is combined with the Delegation Phase, as a manager, new to your company, can introduce specific knowledge and skills that you know are lacking in your company. A new professional manager can be instrumental in formalising the new systems. Note: do not hire on technical knowledge or skills alone – attitude to your company is more important. Can they believe in and commit to the growth of the company?. Allow the new manager to settle in for a few months, giving him the time to pick up on the company culture before letting him loose on the systems. It is not a good idea for the manager to bring exactly the same systems that he was using in his previous company; they may not be suitable for your company. After all, the purpose of the Reactive Phase was to allow the most suitable systems to evolve, eliminating those systems that failed to work for you.

With your adviser in tow, draft a job description showing the areas of responsibility and authority that will be given to the new manager. Avoid drawing the job description too tightly as management jobs tend to change a bit to suit the person doing them. When the new manager is aboard, you will need to work together to reformat the job. The outcomes – the results expected from the appointment of the new manager – should be set out clearly as these are more important than the day-to-day tasks. If the expected result is that the boss has more time to meet customers or is relieved of some tedious duty that he hates doing, then write it down. When grumpiness sets in and you start grumbling about the manager's performance at a later date, the written word will provide evidence of the overall success or failure of the appointment.

The reporting structure must be clear and unambiguous, stating exactly which people report to the new manager and only the new manager. It should also be made clear that the new manager reports to only one boss. The parameters of the authority that the manager has over his people must be set out clearly. Can he reward them and, if so, to what extent? Does he have any sanctions that can be used for control? Can he fire and hire people?

Sometimes, bosses tend to employ managers who are less good than themselves. It seems that the boss feels that he will lose status if he is not regarded by his people as the Delphic Oracle. Commonly he will display signs of jealousy when 'his' people go to the new manager for help and advice. Bosses have to grow up and stop doing the job of a lowly manager; they have more important things to do as the head of the company. Always hire managers who are better than yourself in at least one major area; in that way the company will grow in knowledge, skills and experience and you can safely delegate. You should retain your self-confidence and feel at ease when engaging with managers; asking questions of the manager is better than issuing instructions. The manager will know more than you about his specialist area, but remember that you are the one that can see the bigger picture. But allow them to participate, even in a starring role, in the picture.

After the new manager arrives you must engage in a daily dialogue with him; this is essential in refining the job details and the results expected from him. It will also help to build the mutual trust and confidence of both boss and manager. At the beginning of the relationship you might be afraid that you have made the wrong choice and that the new manager will make mistakes. This is natural and will take a little time to cure, especially as new managers do make mistakes. Your job is to ensure that the mistake is a hole above the waterline, rather than a hole below, one that sinks the ship. The most common mistakes are misunderstanding or not being aware of the exact nature of the human relationships, both within the company and with external stakeholders. The new manager needs time to absorb the culture of the company. All will be well in time.

The whole process may take several months until confidence and trust are gained by all parties. Adjustments in behaviour will need to be made by everybody affected by the new appointment, something that will prove much more difficult for the boss who is used to being in control of everything. Although it can be difficult to accept that you have to adjust your behaviour to accommodate an employee, it will demonstrate that you are reasonable and enhance the mutual confidence between both of you.

The new manager should be expected to improve existing performance so that it produces extra profit to payback more than his cost. The boss can then turn his attention to other things that also improve existing performance. The essence of delegation is that every task should be delegated down the hierarchy to the least costly person that can perform it adequately to the required standard.

You, the boss, must hand over full responsibility and authority to the new manager for his part of the company within a few months. However, you must not abdicate and retire; the art of delegation needs you to take an ongoing interest in the manager's work. Regular formal and informal meetings are still necessary between boss and managers and this contact never ceases. As the boss, you must trust your manager and support him, especially if things go wrong. In particular, support him in the way that he deals with his people in public, whilst reserving the right to correct and advise him in private, if you see something going wrong. Allow for normal human errors, provided they are correctable. Frequently, an existing member of staff will develop a dislike for the new manager; if it comes to the crunch then it is the existing staff member that has to go. As time goes by it will become apparent that some of the people you employed in the early days of the company are no longer suitable for now and the immediate future. You will have to grasp this very painful nettle.

If the manager's staff attempt to go round the manager and go directly to the boss, they should be sent packing and reminded to whom they report. However, it is a good idea for the boss to stay in touch with the lower orders, especially those on the front line, as well as conversing with customers. It has been known for managers to filter information on the way up and on the way down. As the boss, take care that you do not bypass the managers by issuing orders to his people.

Listening to his ideas and encouraging him will be necessary as there is little point in having a manager that cannot improve things. If he cannot improve the company after a reasonable time, then get rid of him. Regardless of the nature of his job, make sure he experiences customer contact, as well as doing some of the front line jobs for a while. A day or two acting as a delivery assistant, with instructions to engage with the Goods-In people at the customers' premises, will broaden his mind and give him a better understanding of the context in which he works. If he can gain the respect of the lower orders then his job as a manager will be a lot easier. Be available for your new manager in order to discuss issues, but do not do his job for him.

Feedback must be made available to the manager relating to all the tasks that he is responsible for and these feedback systems should be developed in a format largely defined by the receiving manager. Informal feedback should be given by you, the boss. If you feedback more or less on a daily basis you can forget the formal annual appraisal systems that are beloved by the bureaucracies. Feedback even a week after the event is probably too distant to be truly effective.

The boss must ensure, as all managers should, that the new manager has all the resources, within normal financial constraints, including training, equipment, time, space and money. The boss has another task which requires some dedication and persuasive ability, and that is to ensure that all departments cooperate fully with each other. This means ensuring an unrestricted flow of information and support for each other. The accounts department, the sales department, the operations department and the delivery folk must talk to each other, informally as well as through the formal links. Cooperation between departments is vital to the survival of the company. If that sounds a little dramatic remember that lack of cooperation between functional departments is predictive of company failure. Try mixing up people from different departments; for example, move the credit controller to the sales department and he will understand the customer better and be able to enlist the support of the sales people when he is collecting in the dosh. When the credit controller reminds the sales people that late payers tend to buy from other companies to avoid 'stops' on deliveries and when they pay up they return to buying from you, there can be considerable cooperation.

Bought Ledger accounts people might be located in or adjacent to the goods inward area where invoices will take on real meaning and dodgy deliveries can be evidenced by their manual colleagues. As the boss, invite people from different departments for a pizza and a bottle or two after work. This is an astonishing reservoir of information for a boss, as well as a very effective way of allowing people to make friends with each other and cooperate across different departments. Encourage your new managers to do the same and they will merge into the company culture more swiftly.

On an aircraft, when the pilot requests the passengers to put on their seat belts they all do so immediately and without negative comment. Likewise, the bus driver reminds people not to stand up until the bus has come to a full stop and again there is no resistance from the passengers. As a boss or as a manager you have similar legitimate power over your people meaning that they will respond to your requests without resistance. So have the confidence to tell your people what to do, but only when necessary; they will almost invariably follow your orders without question.

It sometimes happens that the very first manager that you take on turns out to have been a very good interviewee, but also turns out to be incompetent when in post. Difficult and disappointing as it may be, fire him and immediately set about recruiting another manager. Buy in the best managers you can find; don't compromise or you will surely regret it later. Bosses sometimes worry about the cost of hiring managers if they don't work out and worrying about it makes them think in terms of a full year's associated costs. But you will be able to determine if the manager is right for you within about three months and, in that time he might well have made some productive contribution. If you fire him then, the costs are only for three or four months, less the contribution that he has made during that time.

One of the major points of this book is to ensure that you know, right from the beginning, what is going to be expected of you as you grow. Prepare well in advance for the Delegation Phase, save your pennies specifically for the purpose of paying market value and keep your ears and eyes open for prospective managers that you might approach in the future.

Frequently bosses employ managers who are not quite up to the job and they do so in order to avoid paying market rate salaries. This is a big mistake caused by ignoring the fact that the payback period for a good manager can be expressed in months and not a full year. If the manager is sub-standard, the payback period might be many years, if the appointment ever pays back your investment.

A common mistake is employing your first manager during the Reactive Phase before it has settled down and the processes and systems have not yet evolved sufficiently to become clear. If you do this the manager will flounder and so will you. It will be impossible to develop a job description if the company systems are still in the arms of Doctor Flux. However, you can employ a manager to sophisticate and bed in the systems, effectively combining the Processes Phase with the Delegation Phase; this will work if the new manager knows something about the nature of your company, perhaps with an employment history in similar companies. Remember that your evolved systems are designed to satisfy your needs and imported new systems may not be as effective.

If you think that delegation is very difficult, comfort yourself by looking at some multiple retailers in your location, companies with many stores. Each store has a manager who runs the business on a day-to-day basis. Call in and see the sort of people that can be trusted to run a part of the business without the boss having to look over their shoulder all the time. You will notice that there are thousands of employed managers to whom hundreds of bosses have delegated the responsibility and the necessary authority to run the company business outlets. Put some geographical space between the manager and the boss and the managers cope perfectly well. If you have your processes in place you can feel confident that 'moral hazard' can be limited to acceptable levels.

As a boss you probably find some tasks a duty rather than a pleasure, so delegate them to someone else. If you force yourself to do tedious and taxing tasks using pure unadulterated will power, you will simply exhaust yourself and be too knocked out to deal with the major problem or opportunity that might suddenly appear. You need rest and recuperation after performing a difficult task and if you don't get it you will become a savage beast and upset all the people around you because you lack the will power to act like a nice person. If you like selling and mixing with customers, then do it. If you prefer to don overalls and get your hands dirty, do it. Delegate everything else, except be available for the really high level decisions. If you enjoy your daily routine and don't find it taxing, then you will be better able to deal with major problems or opportunities.

Take care that you do not overtax your people, especially your managers. When they have been engaged in a difficult task for some time, ensure that they follow it with a routine or pleasant task. Make sure all your people have frequent mini rest periods, say about ten minutes every hour. Despite the mini breaks you will find that productivity and accuracy will improve and the added bonus is that everybody will be nicer to everybody else. Emphasise this to customer-facing people, who need rest periods more than most. It is quite difficult to sustain a smiley face all day long without frequent breaks, so allow them to rest and the customers will comment on all the wonderful and helpful people who work in your company. On its own, this could be the differentiation that attracts the customers and allows you to gain better prices.

Taking notice of your people is one of the best motivational techniques available to you. Don't just pass by and say "good morning". Stop and talk with people; ask them questions about their outside interests, as well as their work. Focus on one person at a time, avoiding making little speeches to groups. Don't do it every day but vary it, making it unpredictable to them and diarised to you (otherwise you will forget somebody and they all matter). Irregularity is the rule, as is focusing on one person at a time.

Analysing your people as very important stakeholders in your company is essential. What resources do they bring to you? They are suppliers to your company, bringing their labour so that you can bring your and their ideas and intentions to the market, thereby providing you with a route to success. Analyse each employee as an individual, not as a member of a homogenous group or mass of people. Some will have exceptional, maybe unique, talents or skills and you need to know what they are and how they can be utilised; therein could be found your differentiation that makes the money. Remember the old man in the workshop of the alarms company? He made the company successful by his skill in customising alarms for the customers. Lose him or not recognise his skills and you might lose your differentiation advantage.

If it is easy to find people to work for you, then they will be relatively inexpensive. If the opposite is true and there is a scarcity of the people, the kind you need to employ, then you need to consider your recruitment policies very carefully. You will need a marketing approach including identifying the people you want and approaching them, maybe by email or newsletter, building up a large database of these people. An attractive brand can attract employees as well as customers. Advertising agencies and fashion houses receive a large amount of submissions from would-be employees every day.

Consider if your people can forward integrate and become a rival. If they can do so, consider joining them as an investor, so that their success running their own show can also contribute to your success. What are the expectations of your employees when working for you? Ask them individually, but generally they will expect market value wages and to be treated fairly and with respect. They also value having their ideas for improvements considered seriously. What power do they have over you? They could leave or they could strike or they could sabotage your operations.

What motivates your employees? Firstly, by having their contribution acknowledged, preferably in public, thereby being made to feel that they are an important and valued part of the company. Interview them to find out what particular things would encourage them to be enthusiastic; it may be different for each of them.

There are many sources of information on delegation and managing people and it is suggested that you read several books on the subject, and perhaps attend some training sessions with others of a like mind. Delegation is the most difficult of the administration tasks that you will have to perform if your company is to grow to success, but like everything else, you will get better at it over time.

In the next section of the book there is more on delegation, as used in a different context.

Section 6

Divisions In Extended Markets

Chapter 16

The Fate of the Entrepreneur

Congratulations! You and your managers have grown a company that is fully functional. Your team is in place and working satisfactorily. You are now finding it hard to justify your existence in the business.

You are considering becoming chairman of your local football club. It is probable that your managers and staff are now suggesting, hopefully in diplomatic terms, that you set up an office at home as you will be able to observe the business better and more accurately from a distance. What they are really saying, of course, is, "Get off my patch, I'm trying to do my job and you keep interfering" A very common disease of small companies is a boss who can't let go and continuously hassles his clearly capable managers.

So what does an entrepreneur do now? There is much discussion in academic circles concerning the fate of the entrepreneur as the company reaches a large, formal state. It is said that many entrepreneurs cannot handle the formality of a bigger company and would like to be back at the helm of a smaller, growing company again.

For instance, take a look at Stelios Haji-Ioannou, the charismatic founder of *easyJet*, who has dropped out of his original company but continues to create many more start-ups, including easyInternetcafe, easyCar, easyMoney, easyCinema.

Bobby Hashemi who, along with his sister Sahar, founded *Coffee Republic*, couldn't live with the bureaucracy resulting from their stock market flotation so they dropped out of the company management team. In their book *Anyone Can Do It* (Capstone, 2002), Bobby and Sahar describe reversing into a public company quoted on the Alternative Investment Market, thereby creating the mechanism for raising several million to expand the business. They talk in terms of their roles having "irretrievably changed" and of leaving the company with "feelings of bereavement", a perfect phrase to convey the emotions of leaving a company that one has created.

It sounds wonderful to use the gigantic wealth you have built up, in the company that you founded, to buy a villa in the Sunshine State. But three months lying on a beach or playing tennis would be such a dramatic change from the life that you have become accustomed to whilst running your business, that you will come out in spots. You will spot opportunities everywhere – big ones, little ones, red ones, blue ones. You will get a strange itching sensation in your feet and ankles that even your expensive doctor in Clearwater Beach won't be able to diagnose. Many entrepreneurs have found this out and were drawn back to the daily angst of the small company like a victim to his torturer.

So, what's the cure? You are now at the helm of a successful company, with competent managers in place. Maybe it is time to examine the available options, of which there are many. The examination of these options will be fairly brief, since there are many books available devoted to the subject matter. That is for all except for the final option, which we will examine in greater detail.

Firstly, let us take a look at the option of continuing to grow, focusing on your core business. The proviso here is that the product market sector is large enough to accommodate your continued expansion and that there is still some growth in the sector. Competition will grow more intense if you have to take market share away from competitors. If you go this route, you will probably have to go for domination of the market, becoming *the* largest player in terms of market share. You must do this to achieve the economies of scale necessary to compete successfully in the long term. There are no prizes worth having for second place.

Assuming you are making profits, you will be able to finance your own growth to some extent. If you want to grow very fast then the credibility that you have achieved by your performance to date will allow you to raise capital, either equity investment or long-term loans, to finance your growth. If you keep on growing in the same product market – if you "stick to the knitting" – you will enter the arena of the global players, with all its bureaucracy and all its boredom. Do you want this?

A second, generic, option is to sell the company, and there are several sub-options available here. You can dispose of the company by a trade sale, selling to a competitor, or to someone who wants to enter this particular product market arena. This will often be a long-winded process that will distract you and your senior management team from their daily tasks. If you are selling to a competitor be aware that they may be undertaking research to determine your competitive advantage, at your expense. Do not get too excited at the initial seven or eight figure offer.

If the competitor has an aggressive market stance, as a matter of policy, they might exploit your desire to sell the company by keeping your management fully occupied and running around in non-effective circles. By such means they could do serious damage to your company.

A second sub-option for selling your company is by using a Management Buy-Out (MBO). This means selling to your managers, usually with an external investor providing a substantial part of the funding. Your managers will have to put up lesser sums, but sufficient to demonstrate to the main investor that they have the desirable level of commitment.

Sometimes the opportunity arises for a Management Buy-In (MBI), a third sub-option, which is a variation on the MBO. There are a number of investment banks and venture capitalists that specialise in putting together management teams so that they can take up good investments in the form of buy-in opportunities.

A fourth sub-option is a hybrid version of the MBI and MBO, where perhaps a senior manager within the target company alerts an investment bank to the good opportunity. The bank then adds other necessary managers to form a full team and provides the investment. Inevitably, this hybrid is called a BIMBO.

A fifth sub-option is to float on a recognised stock market, whereby your shares become available to trading by the public. Consequently, shares can be bought in small amounts by many people, thereby limiting their risk. Once you have gained the confidence of the market you will be able to sell all your shares, assuming that your presence at the helm of the company is not the only reason for the market's confidence. Because of the greater number of investors trading on a recognised stock market, the shares in your company become more liquid – they can be bought or sold more easily. Consequently, there can be more competition to buy your shares, therefore the price rises. You can frequently get a better price for your company using this option and, moreover, you can ease yourself out over time.

A third generic option is to liquidate your company and there are two sub-options here. The first sub-option is to run the company down over a period of years, gradually converting all assets into cash and taking it out of the business. Unlike a forced liquidation, in which everything ends up in a fire-sale and is sold for very little, an orderly liquidation can maximise the value of everything in the business.

For the second sub-option for liquidation consider yourself at the end of the growing season. You can now harvest your crop. Stop all investment in the future, vigorously cut out all possible costs and raise your prices. It will take a little while before your customers start to change their allegiance to other suppliers. By which time you will have amassed a large sum of money. Sell off the remaining assets, collect any outstanding debts from your debtors, and put all the money in a big black garbage bag. Then depart for the Virgin Islands.

There are a multiplicity of books and other sources of learning to enable you to continue to grow your company, as long as you focus on your core business. Similarly, there are plenty of books on "How to Sell Your Company" and "How to Float Your Company", and even more advisers to help you achieve those objectives, for a small fee (or, more likely, for a large fee). As for me, I am going to offer you my preferred option, the most natural, most organic, most exhilarating of all – creating 'Divisions In Extended Markets'. Why grow and grow the same business? Seize the day!

If you want to keep that entrepreneurial feeling, that tingle in your loins, that "singin' in the rain" state of mind, then grow more business units. It's more fun to grow many businesses. Become the boss of one of the business units and do it all over again! Where do all these business units come from? Some are growing right there within your existing business.

But you only started one business, so how do the other businesses get there? They originate from customers, they come from employees and they emanate from advisers, colleagues and friends. As the company grows, customers ask for products or services that were not part of the original offer. Rather than upset the customer, the business gives them what they want. After all, the customer is always right, aren't they? If even a small number of customers ask for the same things and those things are different from the core offering, then an embryonic business starts to wiggle its fingers and toes and begins to grow. It cannot be aborted, because the sales manager will fight to keep it. She is, by the nature of her job, wedded to the customers and they must have what they want – a new baby. The customer is the father, occasionally turning up and demanding attention, whilst the sales manager is the mother who will do anything to keep the child alive and well.

There are other parents of other embryonic companies. The bright and enthusiastic young man who comes up with the brilliant idea for another product or service is the mother – the mother of invention? The boss, who unwittingly finds that he is playing the role of 'father', finds himself shelling out to support this infant company.

Here is a real-life scenario taken from a company, called Soltec, which I know well. Soltec's main business is the design and manufacture of lamps for needle-workers, with distribution via retail channels. They have a manager who is married to a beautician. At his prompting they realised that they could design and produce a variety of lamps for beauticians, which they did, using wholesalers as the distribution channel. This constitutes a new and risky business unit – selling new or modified products into a new market, using a new distribution channel. The mother of invention here is an employee.

Over the years, this process of conception within the core business happens a lot. Most new conceptions spontaneously abort, as the attention of the customer or the employee moves elsewhere. Staying with the metaphor of new born babies and their fate, some are born, but shortly after are put out on the barren hillside to perish due to lack of resources to feed them. Others become orphans as their parents move on. Others, due to their intrinsic weaknesses, are deliberately jettisoned, being put in baskets like Moses and floated down the rivers to the great oceans. Mantras like "sticking to the knitting", if strictly adhered to, will act as a form of contraception.

Some of these ideas stick, becoming part of the business. Dallas Cottons is a company that designs bed sheets, pillowslips, eiderdowns and quilts. They outsource the manufacture of the product and sell direct to up-market retailers, including department stores, multiple retailers and single outlet operations. An analysis of their 'sales-by-customer' revealed that, during the previous five years, some 80 up-market hotels had bought bed covers from Dallas Cottons. Dallas had never attempted to sell to hotels, so the fact that the hotels had become customers indicated that 'leakage' had taken place from the marketing promotions. The customer had fathered a new concept business, that of selling product direct to up-market hotels. If they want our bed coverings, what else can we sell them?

Leakage is where promotions targeted at a particular sector also influences the buyers in another sector. New businesses that originate from marketing promotion leakage, bringing in different segments of customers, are extremely valuable. Treated as a separate business they are usually low-risk ventures, since trading is already happening spontaneously. Consequently, you now have direct experience of the business elements and know that they work properly. You have been through the creative, analytical, reactive and systems phases of growth, at least to some extent. Now all you have to do is the empowerment bit, delegating a competent person to develop it.

Artists have a liking for north-facing studios; apparently light from the north is 'cleaner' and less likely to distort colours. When Soltec Lamps was first started by Tony Myers, its sole product market was selling 'cleaner' light bulbs to artists and the only selling technique used was direct, using telemarketing. Fiona, a friend of Tony's, mentioned that people who do embroidery also need to see colours cleanly. In addition, they need to see very small stitches clearly. And, of course, they need to look at a pattern of the piece that they are working on. Soltec designed a lamp with a 'cleaner' bulb and two flexible arms, one holding a large magnifying glass and the other holding a large clip that holds a clipboard with a pattern on it. But telemarketing is an expensive sales technique for relatively low value products directed at individual members of the public. Therefore Soltec started a new (for them) distribution technology by selling to retailers, in large quantities. The public then bought the product from the retailers. Sales of these products now run into many millions and are the core business. And who's the absconded father of this new business – who has planted the seed? A friend called Fiona.

In examining your existing business you may notice unexpected successes or failures. Like the unexpected customer type or the request for an unusual product or variation on an existing product. Once upon a time local retailers used to keep a 'wants' list on their counters, noting down these odd requests. When enough requests for a particular product had been received they would buy in the product and test it for sales potential. If successful, it would be adopted as a regular stock item.

Is your product doing for the customer what you think it is doing? They might be using it in a particular way that has never occurred to you. Tony Myers, of Soltec Lamps, does not engage in embroidery. Consequently, he made the false assumption that such a hobby is always performed on a table. When you think about it, most indoor hobbies engaged in by men, such as model ship building, stamp collecting and making cathedrals out of matchsticks, are performed on a bench or table. All the photographs and illustrations used in the marketing of Soltec lamps showed women doing embroidery at a table. It took a few years and the introduction of the first couple of focus groups to find out that many women, maybe most, embroider sitting in a comfortable armchair or on a sofa. The design team went into overdrive, creating floor-standing lamps and changing the illustrations on the packaging, on the fliers and in the catalogues. Had a potential competitor spotted the real context of usage before Soltec, they could have become a serious challenger.

Stay aware of the context of usage of your products. Your company may supply a product for a particular application but the user may have a different purpose in mind. Video cassette players were introduced into the home in the 1970s as a device for time-shifting of your favourite TV programs. This sounds like a very useful purpose. But what really drove the astonishing rate of adoption by the public of video recorders? The real reason was the new-found ability to distribute and watch movies, without the fuss of going to the cinema or setting up 8mm projectors and other paraphernalia.

All sorts of products made for a particular purpose suffer a change of context from that which the designer intended. Coffee mugs are used to hold pens and pencils and shaving gear. Oven dishes are on night tables holding small change, keys, wallets and all the other stuff that a man tries to fit onto a too-small night table when he gets home. Why an oven dish? Because it's tough and doesn't break, especially when he gestures broadly during his dream of delivering the State of the Union address. Any unusual discoveries in relation to context of use can expose a new, already operational, business.

Unexpected failures are more difficult to unravel. If you can determine the cause of a failure the learning will be huge, possibly leading to a major breakthrough. Failure of an established product offering is often due to a substitute offering. Something better has appeared on the market that is displacing your offer. Find it, adopt it and improve it. The sellers of typewriters for the most part allowed themselves to go bust rather than adopt the computerised word-processor as their main product line.

It is not just differences in products and market segments that you should investigate. A change in the distribution chain is equally important. The Internet is an obvious one. People are no longer demanding a branch of their bank on the high street or in the shopping centre. They have switched to on-line banking in droves. The Internet is the distribution chain for information and it has had a profound effect on the retail distribution chain. Although Amazon.com do not distribute product via the Internet, they do distribute marketing and sales information. On-line shopping carts substitute for the conventional high street or shopping mall retailer. The method of distribution of the product is different. Instead of going to the retail outlet and taking your purchase home in the car it is now delivered by an Amazon carrier right to your door. Half a century ago it was common practice to telephone your grocer at 10 a.m. to order your list of provisions and receive delivery at your home in the afternoon. It's called 'the wheel of retailing'. Even today's shopping mall is similar to a medieval town's market, complete with entertainers.

A change in geographic area of operations can, in itself, create a new business. A London-based merchant, John Wren, has built a multi-million pound business selling tools to local tradesmen in south London. That part of London has a high immigrant population and alerted by an African customer to what financiers describe as an arbitrage opportunity, they started selling tools in bulk to distributors in Nigeria. It was cheaper for distributors in Nigeria to buy branded tools from John Wren in London than directly from the manufacturer. Thus a new business was created, with a new area of operations, a new distribution chain and a new market segment. The directors did not intend to create a new business; they simply seized an opportunity to increase sales revenue. Unfortunately, as you will see below, they did not treat it as a new and different business. They integrated into their existing business of retailing tools to local tradesmen.

When a company has been going for some years it will have accumulated a number of these cuckoo-in-the-nest businesses. You will notice that the metaphor has now changed, from human babies to avian babies, for reasons that will soon become apparent. The more directors of the business there are, the more cuckoo fledglings there will be. The number of cuckoo chicks is a product of the age of the company in years, multiplied by half the number of directors. Don't you just love business school pseudo-science?

Another company (let's call it Starling) that I know well, has been trading for over 20 years, with two founder directors still in place and two other directors of about 12 years standing. All four directors are shareholders in the company. The core business is retailing from multiple stores. They have a small factory, created in response to difficulties in obtaining supplies of a particular range of products. They have a property company, created to rent out the spaces above their shops. They have a publishing company of periodicals targeted at their retail customers, created so that their advertising budget could be spent in house. They have a wholesaling company, justified by the extra discounts they obtain from suppliers by buying larger quantities at a time. In addition, they have a mail-order company, taking orders over the telephone and dispatching products to distant customers. In an entirely different location they have a web-based sales company, taking orders online and despatching products to distant customers.

Viewed from inside the company, it's a nightmare. From outside the company, from a spectator's point of view, it's a hilarious Keystone Kops movie. The directors are being pushed and pulled in all directions at once and board meetings resemble tag wrestling matches. They balance buckets of paint on partially open doors so that the next director to arrive at the board meeting will display his true colours. But remember, we're now talking cuckoos, those birds that lay their eggs in other birds' nests. After the cuckoo egg hatches it tries to force the other non-cuckoo eggs out of the nest. The cuckoo fledgling is greedy and demands that the foster parents use all their resources to provide it with a constant supply of food, leaving any other fledglings to starve.

Each business in the Starling nest has a foster parent in the form of a director and each director is intent on securing as much of the common resources as he can, in order to feed his particular cuckoos. The result is fairly predictable. Roughly (I use the word advisedly) equal and opposite forces lead to a standstill.

Overheads shoot up regularly and spasmodically like Old Faithful, the Yellowstone Park geyser, as each director hires more people and overspends on advertising budgets. More importantly, even essential tasks are forgotten or ignored. Whilst sales revenue increases the company profits decrease.

My observation, over several hundreds of companies, is that companies trying to run several businesses as if they were one, seriously under-perform. As the company continues to grow and more ideas get put into practice the complexity of the company increases and management is no longer able to make clear-cut decisions. Every decision seems to be good for one part of the company but bad for another part. Arguments between the directors and between the managers of the company increase in frequency and intensity. Since no decisions can be agreed on, the company comes to a standstill. Firstly, profits decline, to be followed shortly by a levelling off of sales revenue increases and then a standstill in revenue. If this coincides with a market change, such as an increase in the intensity of competition or the introduction of a substitute product from outside the existing product market arena, then the company starts showing losses and may go bust.

A few years ago I witnessed the demise of a 40 year old company; let's call it Magnus & Sons.

The old man had founded and created a multi-million pound company and, on retirement, passed it on to his two sons. The sons had had an easy life as a result of the business profits created by Daddy. When the sons took over as the senior executives, they had a competition within the business to see who could create the largest royal court. They had two private offices each, with each office being large enough to comfortably accommodate four people. They ignored analyses produced by their accountant showing that several parts of the business were loss making. They added on extra people to their favourite bits of the company, regardless of profitability. One of the directors kept repeating the mantra "Our problem is F.T.I., failure to implement", with a smile, as they sunk under the waves.

Why did this happen? My view is that the founding father had built up the large, profitable company over several decades. For all that time he was the sole active director of the company and it was his decision alone to foster some fledgling businesses. Because they were added slowly and infrequently over 35 years, the founder understood the way they fitted into the business. There being only one director, there were no arguments about resource allocation or strategic direction.

Enter the two sons. The complexity of the company that had been left to them would fox anyone without formal training in analysis of companies. They didn't understand the company, they were scared of the unknown and they had no experience in decision making. Their idea of how to be a boss was gained from films like *The Hudsucker Proxy*, the one where Paul Newman and Tim Robbins are sitting in an office the size of a football pitch.

What was the solution that the two Magnus sons came up with? Fundamentally, the right one – simplify the business to the extent that they could understand and control it. Lacking the analytical skills and under some psychological pressure from the mere presence of the old man, they were unable to do a tidy-up job. To escape the personal stress they had to kill it all off and start a more simple business, which is exactly what they have done. They projected the causes of the company failure very skilfully onto their employees, their competitors, their suppliers and the state of the economy, thereby saving their self-esteem. This explains their cheerfulness as they rode towards what most of us regard as the Valley of Death, a creditors' liquidation. Two months later they had opened a small business, a miniscule version of the failed business and they seemed very happy and more motivated.

Do you enjoy crossword puzzles? Many people involved in decision-making in business find crosswords relaxing. Crosswords might be very taxing on the mind and you might have to stretch a lot to find the right answer to the clue. But when you do find the right word you know that it is the right word and, if the compiler is any good, no other word can be substituted. There is a clear cut answer and when you've made your decision you know that you are right. The problem that you have solved is contained within a closed system, with a finite number of variables, all of which are known to you, assuming you are fluent in the language. Solving this sort of problem is satisfyingly finite.

Business problems exist within a comparatively open system, a system of great complexity. The number of variables that impinge on a decision is not known and consequently all business decisions have to be based on incomplete information. You can never be absolutely sure that your decisions are right. But we must go there, into the unknown, making decisions and covering our asses in case of a bad downside result. So, how do we unravel the complexity of the grown up company whose children have not yet left home?

We have to firstly determine if there is more than one business operating within the company as a whole. That requires us to define the essential constituents of a business. What elements constitute a business? Many people will answer that it is a product and a market, just that. But there is more to a business than just those two elements.

Let us assume that selling books (the product) to domestic readers (the market) is a business. Further, let us compare Amazon.com with any High Street book retailer, asking the question: are they in the same business?

For a start, the customer purchasing experience is distinctly different. Some people value the experience of shopping in a retail bookshop, where they can physically browse the bookshelves, never knowing what they are going to find. They might sit on a sofa or have a coffee whilst reading bits of books. They will frequently purchase a book that they didn't know existed until they went into the shop. High street retailers like Barnes & Noble and Waterstones satisfy these customers with their network of stores.

To other types of customers, the prospect of going out to the shops is viewed as a negative experience. In some cases the shops may appear to be too far away. If you live in Leroy, in central Montana, you are not likely to drive several hundred miles to Great Falls just to browse the bookstores. Other customers, with an interest in reading about a specific subject, are more easily satisfied by finding their books from catalogues or by recommendations from others with the same interest. Again, people who are short of time will buy over the Internet and have their books delivered to their door. These are the people that Amazon.com will satisfy.

And, of course, consumer behaviour is both variable and unpredictable. The same customer might go to the shops today and tomorrow click online and buy from Amazon.

The difference between Amazon and the high street shop retailer, in terms of the elements of a business, is in the technology used – the internet and the physical distribution system (both are technologies), replacing the traditional high street stores. If it is claimed that these differences are slight, and that product and market are the essential elements, then why does Amazon dominate the net-based book market? It seems that the technology required to run a chain of high street bookshops is demonstrably different from the technologies used by Amazon. Otherwise, the retail bookshops would dominate the web-based market. Amazon has climbed the learning curve in these two technologies – physical distribution and distribution of marketing information – faster than any competitor and without a previous history of book retailing to build upon. In fact, one might conclude that previous retailing of books from a high street store was a disadvantage when it comes to operating an online bookstore. A disadvantage based on an industry-wide recipe, the practice of which is so common that the players in the industry are not even aware of the paradigm within which they are operating.

So far, we have three elements that can be combined to create a business:

product, market, distribution system. We can further define a fourth element, 'technology', as the operational core of the business such as construction, engineering or graphic design. In the same sense, Amazon is an 'internet retail' technology business, as distinct from a 'stores retail' business; both sell directly to the consumer public.

The fifth element that defines a business is its geographical area of operations. There are a number of reasons why a business must define this area. Firstly, there are cultural reasons. If the business designs and makes bikinis for the South American market, it will certainly not be able to operate the same business in the Muslim countries of the Middle East, where modesty of dress for women is a core cultural value. Food products, especially in respect of the main family meal, will also present difficulties in crossing cultural boundaries. Differences in languages will inhibit expansion into other countries, although this tends to be a psychological problem of the management rather then a real barrier. Hi-tech physical items such as cars, earth moving equipment, computers and hi-fi equipment will have little difficulty in crossing cultural borders.

Secondly, the density of potential customers within an area will determine whether that area is included, taking into account the density of suppliers in the same area. You know that one – you really do not want to try and sell sun tanning lamps to those living in Ghana, based on the fact that there are no competitors in that market.

A third reason why the area of operations must be defined is that geographical features, such as mountain ranges and other inhospitable terrain can inhibit distribution. A supermarket based on the Mediterranean coast of Turkey is unlikely to accept home delivery orders from domestic customers living on the coast of the Black Sea because transport across the vast mountain range is both costly and time consuming.

You may wish to expose other elements, if you judge them to be relevant. For instance, sourcing and the supply chain might be useful. However, for our purposes, we will accept that five elements constitute a business. Here are a couple of examples of businesses:

To provide books (*the product*)
By internet retailing *(technology)*
And home deliveries *(distribution)*
To the domestic reader (*the market)*
In the UK (*area of operations*)

To provide a repair service (*the product*)
Through plumbing *(technology)*
And site-visiting engineers (*distribution)*
To commercial organisations *(the market)*
In Delaware (*area of operations*)

Any change of one or more of these five elements might create a business that can stand alone. And, maybe more importantly, *should* stand alone.

In the second example shown above, the company has been receiving many calls from domestic customers in Delaware, its chosen geographical area of operations, with requests to deal with their plumbing problems. Although the company's target market is commercial organisations, marketing leakage to domestic customers has taken place because the engineers' vans are sign-written with the company name and contact details.

The company accepts the domestic calls and, consequently, they are now dealing with two different markets – commercial and domestic. The cuckoo has laid the egg in the nest and it is different from the existing egg. Let battle commence. The commercial market demands parts and service for urinals and sanitary towel disposal units, not usually found in domestic properties. The domestic market demands parts and service for baths and fancy showers, not usually found in commercial premises. Sourcing for the new market is different, but easily solved. However, the engineers vans cannot carry a full stock of domestic parts as well as commercial parts. Which business gets preference in respect of the resource of van space?

Domestic customers get more stressed out when they have plumbing problems, so the engineers and desk-based controllers will need the personal communications skills to pacify this new type of customer. Which business gets more than its fair share of the time resource?

The company makes little effort to attract more domestic customers and continues to accept only those customers that result from marketing leakage. They do not really want to get into advertising, preferring to stick to their direct mail system that brings in commercial customers with the minimum of marketing cost.

They are now operating two businesses and conflicts will arise in terms of allocation of engineers. Given a commercial emergency and a domestic emergency and only one available engineer, which customer gets the service? The fledgling cuckoo – the domestic customer – is making the loudest noise, 'cos she's very stressed out, so the controller gives in and directs the engineer there. This endangers the retention of a much more valuable commercial customer. Different markets create different businesses.

Different products also create different businesses. Plumbing engineers are frequently trained in gas engineering and always have a smattering of electrical knowledge. They are perfect recruits for a company servicing gas-fired pizza ovens. It is a short step from commercial plumbing to commercial oven maintenance. Apart from the sourcing of parts, very little changes. This is a very tempting cuckoo, indeed.

We have seen that a change in distribution *technology* – from retail shop to home delivery – fundamentally changes the nature of a business and the skills required to run that business. Changing from retail shop to party plan selling in peoples' homes also creates a new business. Changing distribution chain from supplying wholesalers to supplying retailers will create a new business, too.

The time has come to expose the different businesses masquerading as one business. The outing hour is here. The next step is to analyse your company in an attempt to isolate different businesses.

You might be able to spot the different businesses operating within the company fairly easily, but if you are not familiar with the company you might have to do a little analysis. If you do, start with an analysis of the customer base, segmenting the customers in whatever way you feel is appropriate. Attach to each segment the products that they buy, the technology used and the distribution chain. That should show up some different businesses, if they exist. Use a columnar analysis or a mind mapping technique or write the different elements on cards so that you can shuffle them about. Whatever you use, bear in mind that this is not a scientific analysis. Immediately you start to put customers into segments you are forced to make assumptions, and the assumptions are based on you very own unique subjective opinion.

Deal likewise with geographic area selection. The fact that there is a political border, a state line, between Delaware and Maryland may not be relevant to your business. So use your gut feel and common sense to decide whether this or that combination is a business. At this stage we are not concerned whether the business might be a viable economic entity or not.

The primary purpose is to expose the businesses that do not sit happily together. This especially applies to those businesses that compete for the resources of peoples' time, money, space or anything else that matters. Take the effect on the brand into account. Different categories of product being offered under the same brand can be confusing for the customer and consequently damaging for the brand.

When you have exposed the separate businesses what do you do then? If you plan to concentrate on your core business and grow into a very large company, then you must cut out the distracting businesses and abandon them.

If you want to have some entrepreneurial fun, stay with me through the next chapter and turn those cuckoos into soaring golden eagles.

Chapter 17

Gather Ye Rosebuds

"Roll up, roll up" they cry, "we will unleash the creative power of your people and lead you to the promised land of economic success"

Exhortations to be creative and innovate fill the pages of hundreds of business books and magazines. Such cries for change are amplified by thousands of consultants who will teach you and your people to be ever more creative in running your business. Then one day you succumb and decide to send your people on a course to unleash their creativity.

Some might never come back. They have been unleashed and, having bought a beret and a striped T-shirt, they have gone to set up their easel in Montmartre, in Paris, France.

But the ones that got away are not the problem. It's all those who come back wanting to apply their creativity and who get very upset when they are not allowed to do so. Just imagine your entire workforce simultaneously being creative. Your Cybernauts stand shoulder to shoulder defending the bridge, but they finally give way to the creative hordes. Your carefully honed processes, based on years of reacting to the subtleties of the marketplace, are razed and more creative ideas are imposed.

Unfortunately, nobody thought of informing the customers. But who cares? Everybody knows that customers are just a staid old bunch of habit-forming zombies. After all, they just keep on buying the same old brands, like junkies. Try to change the nature or look of your product and they are immediately up in arms.

Look back to the Processes phase, when we laid down the guidelines that allow us to turn the handle on the money-making machine and produce profits. If you remember, we allowed at that time for the formation of a team of Cybernauts, the people who ensure that our systems do not get out of date. The Cybernauts introduce incremental changes continuously as required for the benefit of the stakeholders in the business.

Do not allow the desire to be seen as an exciting, creative genius to adversely affect your judgement here. Do not mess with your systems, processes or technocracy that together ensure your trading activities are turned into profit. Incremental changes in products and processes will always be necessary to lead the pack in selected areas and to stay with the pack in other areas. But real innovation, the sort that leaps the competition in a single bound, comes from recognising and creating new businesses.

By the way, I have no objections to companies sending their people on creativity courses. It is an excellent antidote to boredom at work – insurance companies do it all the time, although they take care not to over-excite their actuaries who might need to lie down in a darkened room after experiencing the course.

Recognise that for many people their work serves a very basic purpose – to feed, clothe, house and protect themselves and their families. The stability provided by predictable work allows them to be more adventurous outside work. If you want to experience fear and the challenge of confronting it, you could go bunjy-jumping or snowboarding high up in the Rockies. Most people cannot do this sort of thing without a stable routine in some other part of their life.

Innovation is not an end in itself. Innovation in a business context has to provide a competitive advantage of some sort. The existence of organic business units within your existing company, ones that have grown without effort on your part, indicate that there is a market for a product or service that is not being satisfied by existing suppliers. The customers have discovered you and consider you as the best people to satisfy their needs. This is true innovation.

The term "business unit" generally describes a part of a business that functions, on a day-to-day basis, with some degree of autonomy. A manufacturing company with several geographically dispersed factories, each with its own manager and support staff, will describe each factory as a business unit. Similarly, a multiple retailer, with a chain of retail outlets, could describe each outlet as a business unit.

These business units use the same processes, governed by the company's technocrats, and the same strategies. They do not have the freedom, the degree of autonomy, to create their own strategies.

Consider the development of a business unit allowing its managers to diverge from the strategies of the core business. This 'strategic business unit' now has the freedom to create its own new strategies. It can change its product offer so that it is different from that of the parent company. Moreover, it can change its markets, technology, distribution methodology and its geographic area of operations. If it can do all these things it can truly innovate.

Many entrepreneurs, over several years, have created profitable steady growth businesses, paying a good salary to the owner manager. Then a common problem arises; they get bored, bored, bored. To relieve the boredom, in some cases, they create problems just in order to solve them. In many cases they start to damage their own companies by interfering with the work of their managers. If the problem isn't solved after a year or two they start to consider selling the business and many of them do so, in the belief that they can start another business from scratch. There are some examples of successful serial entrepreneurs, but most entrepreneurs cannot repeat the success of their first business. The failure rate is the same as first-time starters, but the money from the sale of the first company allows many more attempts.

The solution to boredom, perhaps obviously, is to create a new and dynamic business by spinning off a strategic business unit from the existing business. It can be run at a pace to suit the manic, Formula 1, adrenalin junkie, risk-taking boss. Or the entrepreneur can set a pace more like fishing from a river bank on a warm day.

So, the first great benefit of creating a new strategic business unit is that it brings the boss back to life, with all the physical and psychological benefits that go with it. The managers of the existing business benefit, as well – the boss isn't leaning over their shoulder quite so often.

A second benefit of creating a strategic business unit from an integrated business is gained from the reduction in complexity within the main business. Managing becomes easier, decisions are made faster, the culture and feel of the business is less contentious. This is usually followed by increased profitability or growth, or both if the rate of growth is kept in check.

An integrated business that is different from the core business seldom produces proper profits. In many instances these cuckoos in the nest are losing money. In cutting them out, the main company increases its profitability. When cut out and turned into a strategic business unit, the cuckoo business either becomes profitable or it goes bust. In either case, the parent company will be better off. It's a non-zero sum game that is very beneficial.

An integrated business, one different from the core business, will perform better when trading as a strategic business unit, due to the increased motivation of those working within it. Group identification will bond the people in the business into a cooperative team. They will want to out-perform other business units and show off their prowess generally. They will be less bureaucratic than the main company and consequently more responsive to the needs of their customers. It is probable that they will grow much faster than they did as an integrated business.

The more strategic business units you can create, the more step innovation you will generate, rather than the gradual slope of incrementalism. The resultant group of companies becomes truly innovative and more flexible in response to competitive pressures.

If strategic business units are formed as separate limited liability companies, the parent company reduces risk by spreading its bets. Provided, of course, that there are no cross-company guarantees given (check out the tax position on group companies). In addition, cash flow can be improved by raising investment for an individual strategic business unit from external investors or partners.

Strategic business units can be sold off separately, without damaging the whole business group. This can provide an exit route for retiring shareholder managers or for external investors. If it is desirable to keep the business unit within the group rather than sell it off, then a buy-back of shares by the group can allow retirees or investors to exit whilst realising their investment.

To allow (I use the word deliberately) a strategic business unit to succeed, consider the analogy of your successor, your son. You nurture him, providing food, shelter and protection through the early days. You send him to school and educate him. At the age of 18 he goes off to college, leaving home for the first time.

Instead of engaging with his parents on a daily basis he now engages with college lecturers and a new peer group of fellow students. Occasionally, he returns home, with a pillow case full of dirty washing, whilst reporting to you on his progress. If you are in the habit of offering advice on how he should live his life you will find yourself increasingly ignored. But tell him to do his own washing at college; encourage independence in your children.

If everybody copied their parents' behaviour then there would be no progress. Once upon a time somebody's son left the troglodyte cave, built himself a house and, despite the protests of his parents, went to live there. His peer group copied him and a new generation moved on. A new generation that you will never get to know as well as your son does. The world keeps changing, despite tradition, leaving behind those who do not change to accommodate the new environment.

Remember the Empowerment Phase stuff in section five? Well, you're going to need it when cutting out a strategic business unit that will be run by a manager appointed by you. You will have to select a self-motivated individual to act as managing director; make no compromises, get the best. Given enough freedom, they will become independent fairly soon, especially if you starve them a little.

Cutting out a strategic business unit whilst it is still in the Reactive Phase may result in more failures. But, because in this phase it is more flexible and lighter on its feet, the successes can be spectacular. Cutting out a strategic business unit after the Processes Phase is a safer bet, since all systems have been proven already. But it may turn out to be less extraordinary in its performance.

How do we increase the chances of success for any particular strategic business unit? Without doubt, the most important element is the selection of the managing director for the strategic business unit. In addition to management skills they will need to have experience and knowledge of the customer base and, above all, a desperate desire to be the best. All this implies that they will be familiar with the geographic area of sales operations because the cultures of customers tend to be geographically based.

Conversely, the geographical distances between cultural differences can be very short. In a multiple retail company I knew well, trading nationwide in the UK, there were very distinct differences between London and Newcastle, a distance of only a few hundred miles. These differences surfaced as customer acceptance of prices, colours and style variations of the product range.

The managing director for the strategic business unit will need at least some knowledge of the technologies being used, if not a complete understanding. However, it is generally better to have a managing director skilled in sales then a technologist as head of the unit. This doesn't mean, of course, that a technologist cannot be a skilled salesperson. But the emphasis must be on staying close to the customer and interacting with them.

The manager will need to be motivated by achievement. In addition, you will need to motivate by other means, including financial rewards.

Work out a financial structure for the new company, one that ensures a substantial long-term reward for the new managing director. This reward has a long-term payback to ensure that investment for the future is made in the business by the managing director. This does not mean merely re-investment of cash profits. It means investment of time and maybe other resources in building relationships for future benefit. It means being patient in establishing long-term relationships with customers, having first put a value on the customer by forecasting their potential spend over the next five years or so. It means investing time and retained profits in developing products patiently, not diving in too early attempting to make a fast buck.

The objective of the managing director of the new strategic business unit must be to create a company with a saleable future value which makes his share worthwhile.

Most intelligent managers realise that a minority shareholding in a private company, dominated by a majority shareholder, is worthless. A gain on shares can usually only be made when the company is sold. The value of shares in a small company, one that has a number of shareholders but no single majority shareholder, is higher. Provided that any shareholders' agreement is not too restrictive, there can be a small market in those shares. There are, of course, some tiny stock markets in operation, run by stockbrokers or others, who might well list the company. There is a strong case to be made for the benefits that come from reducing your own shareholding to a less than majority amount. Such a shareholding structure can be motivating to a manager with a share options earn out.

As a person, you cannot really manage more than one company at any one time. Consequently you might consider selling off shares in the strategic business units that you create, to a level that you no longer have a majority shareholding. Not only will you get some money from the sale of these shares, but you can select the additional potential shareholders by what they have to offer to the company to help it on its way to success. And, with no dominant shareholder, all involved will be more motivated to help the company.

The promise of rewards in the distant future is motivating in an intellectual sort of way. Emotionally, deferred gratification does not come naturally to most people. It only comes to the surface when one has the time to contemplate the situation and make a few calculations. More immediate rewards are necessary to motivate people on a daily basis.

Agree an employment contract that pays out frequent rewards based on performance. If the rewards come predictably every month, then fairly soon they will be accepted as a right, not a reward. If that happens, the rewards will fail to motivate, but their absence will cause considerable demotivation.

Short term rewards should operate like a Las Vegas slot machine – giving frequent small rewards, interspersed with periods of no reward. Infrequently, a large reward should be given, almost unpredictably. Year end bonuses are conventionally large, infrequent, but usually quite predictable. Try using moving annual totals as a basis for bonus. Calculations based on the previous twelve months' performance can pay out at any month end provided the target has been achieved for the previous twelve months. This discourages the slow start to the year, which is usually encouraged by the thought that "I can make it up in the second half and still make bonus".

Such rewards can be used to allow the managing director to acquire shares in the strategic business unit. An earn-out ratchet system will effectively dispense shares, over the years, as each previously agreed performance level is reached.

Do not base rewards on sales revenue. The managing director of the strategic business unit has the power to set the pricing policy. Even if you try to retain control over this element, you can't – it is easily circumvented. If the rewarded targets are based on sales revenue, such targets are easily achieved by discounting prices, cutting deeper and deeper, until the target is achieved. Invoices can be put through in advance of delivery or held back, in order to maximise rewards. From time to time, the short term rewards will be more powerful motivators than the long term reward and the strategic business unit manager will rationalise by telling himself that he can collect the maximum payout here, then move to another employer.

Do not base rewards on net profits. The new strategic business unit will be expected to grow and there is a trade-off between growth and net profit. In order to grow there needs to be a re-investment of profits in marketing effort. That includes not only sales promotion, but research and development for new products, packaging, distribution systems, branding and so on. Recast the management accounts layout to show 'net profits' before marketing expenditure of all types – NPBMktg. This will show what profits could be made if a strategy of consolidation were introduced (cutting down marketing spend) which is very helpful in demonstrating value to a potential buyer of the company.

Sales revenue is certainly vanity – it can be achieved easily by selling at a price considerably less than the competitors. Through force of habit virtually all companies address their sales targets first, prompted by the fact that accounting calculations put sales revenue on the top line. Yet sales revenue is only a means of creating gross profit. So put gross profit as the top line and then use the available options to achieve it – price increase, sales growth, reduction in direct labour and buying-in costs. Why keep chasing your tails – oops, meant to say sales – when a tiny price increase or cost reduction can achieve the same effect at virtually no cost?

Returning to the managing director of the new strategic business unit, it should be clear that short-term rewards should be based not on sales revenue performance, but on gross profit. That will ensure that eyes are kept firmly focused on the most important gateways to profitable growth.

The managing director has the power to control spending on overheads and the personal objectives of managers are not always in line with the objectives of shareholders (that is a polite way of putting it). A Lear jet is a thing of beauty, a very desirable possession. But is it really necessary to own your own airline when you only make a dozen flights a year? The only way to handle this is to create a contract that is specific in its restrictions on spending of the sort that might yield a personal gain for the manager, his family or friends and associates, but contributes nothing to the company shareholders.

Allow the manager of the strategic business unit to select his own employees. His immediate need is to form a team who respond to him, acknowledging his legitimate authority to lead and swearing loyalty to the company. But, in the light of the preceding paragraph, beware of nepotism. You do not really want the manager's entire extended family working for the company.

The managing director of the strategic business unit must have complete autonomy, in all matters of tactics and strategy. Think of your son – if you try to run his life for him, making all his decisions for him, he will surely become depressed, turn to drugs and drink, ending up on skid row.

However, every managing director should listen to advice and decide whether to adopt it or not. Ensure that a bunch of stage hands is available, of a composition suited to the phase of growth that the strategic business unit is going through. Remember, your interests and those of the managing director of the strategic business unit are fairly well aligned and, generally speaking, what he does for himself will almost invariably benefit you. Always provided you have written a contract that keeps excessive personal benefits in check.

Ensure that reporting systems are put in place so that you are informed on a regular basis, say monthly. Concentrate on the gross profit element. Design in moving annual total graphs to clearly show trends in labour productivity, the cost of bought in materials, gross profit, overheads and net profit. Sales marketing reports should include graphs showing trend in sales, prices, customer stability, customer turnover, customer value per annum, average transaction value, customer satisfaction levels and brand perception.

The most important element of such reports is to focus the management of the strategic business unit on the important elements affecting the business, of which there may be many other factors of importance not mentioned above. The secondary function of such reports is to keep the appropriate advisers informed so that their advice is relevant.

Although the convention is to have board meetings of directors only, go beyond this. Have monthly meetings to include a mix the stage hands, which should, of course, have members from outside the group of companies. Due to the legal responsibility that directors carry, they have to be careful about what they say, consequently tending to be conservative in their opinions. Others can give their opinions freely, which is what is really needed.

Such monthly meetings serve an invaluable purpose in that they provide motivation for the managing director of the SBU. It is an opportunity for him to show off to a captive audience. Because he has to be on stage every month he will make every effort not to appear to have forgotten his lines. The meeting is an opportunity to verbally reward the manager for good performance. In line with rewards occasionally and unpredictably being omitted, a kick in the ass every now and then will work motivational wonders. Just make sure that the kicking is done by different people at different meetings, otherwise a case of "he's got a down on me" paranoia develops in the manager, which is definitely not motivating.

Applying again the analogy of the son leaving home, there is some need to separate the strategic business unit geographically. There is frequently a father-son relationship between a CEO and the management team of a strategic business unit. Sons must learn from their peers, not their parents, if they are to survive and thrive in their world. For the new strategic business unit to be truly independent and to develop into an adult company, it is desirable to separate father and son.

At this point, if someone mentions the phrase "portfolio management" to you, I suggest that you run away at a fast canter. If they suggest that you consider "horizontal strategies", increase your pace to a gallop.

Portfolio management refers to managing a portfolio of companies or products and making investments and resource decisions in relation to each individual unit. It treats the business units as a group that needs group management and consequently limits the strategic freedom of each unit.

Horizontal strategies, part of portfolio management, refer to the sharing of resources between the units in the portfolio, in order to benefit from synergies. Remember the plumbers in Delaware? We will come back to these strategies a little later.

When cutting out new businesses try to make sure that they can fund themselves fairly quickly. Do not over-invest in a new strategic business unit. Large dollops of cash are toxic when placed at the disposal of the relatively inexperienced managers of small companies. Like athletes on performance-enhancing drugs, they become dependent on the supply instead of making use of their own assets. When the supply dries up they are forced back on to their own resources and fail to achieve.

Think about 'bomber crews', small groups of people that bond into tight, cohesive units when faced with adversity. Adversity is a superb motivator for groups; it turns every day into a challenging adventure, whilst enabling the group to manoeuvre with the fluidity of a flock of birds. Give them too much in the way of resources, take away the challenge, and they become fat and satisfied and increasingly less productive. The approach must be to keep them on survival rations and force them to fend for themselves.

In practice, when entrepreneurs put cash into strategic business units it is almost invariably in order to bail them out, not for the purpose of gaining an increase in return on investment. Let the strategic business unit create its cash flow in the ways that are normal to small companies, such as clever working capital management and short-term bank borrowing.

But supposing they fail? If they do, just remember where they came from; they weren't doing much good there, cluttering up your core business. Besides, if you have noted the guidelines of the preceding paragraphs, you won't have invested all that much cash in them.

Some will fail. But others will triumph and grow big and strong and valuable. Try adopting the attitude of the professional managers of venture capital providers. They do not expect every one of their investments to succeed and they probably expect most to fail. But they are confident that the few winners will more than make up for the failures.

When I mentioned earlier that you should break into a fast canter when somebody mentions "portfolio management" this is what I was driving at. Avoid corporate planning, emanating from your head office. If central management is applied, the most likely result is that the strategic business unit will become stifled. At head office, you are too far away from the marketplace to produce intelligent design of plans and there is nothing that head office can offer the business unit that they can't get elsewhere. There are plenty of banks that will provide strategic business units with cash loans, if they can demonstrate their ability to service the interest charges. If the business unit cannot do so, then they shouldn't have any cash.

The advisors and stage hands can provide the management of the strategic business unit with strategic options. The boss of the unit can decide on what options to take up, in consultation with his own team, as necessary. So there is no need to consider whether corporate planning should be top down or bottom up or some mix of the two. Just let them get on with it. Come to think of it, that's bottom up, isn't it?

Please do not upset the strategic business units by putting them into separate categories and calling them rude names. Names such as 'star', 'cash cow', 'problem child' and 'dog' are very subjective descriptions, and the techniques for categorising business units in this way are very subjective. The techniques depend largely on a forecast of the future in terms of performance. And, if we can forecast the future with accuracy, then professional fund managers wouldn't get it wrong much of the time. If you describe one of your business units as a "problem child" they just might become one. Give a dog a bad name, and all that.

If you milk your cash cow and give the money to some other business unit, what do you think the motivational effect will be on the managers of the cattle ranch? Their newly born calves will starve, because cash cows are not allowed to invest their own cash. Behave in this way in respect of one of your business units and they might become mavericks and try to escape the herd. Other business units might behave like sheep and remember, that when sheep wake up each morning, their first comment is "Oh, dear. I'm still alive"

If you want to play the investment game, there are plenty of well controlled stock markets around the world. Go there and have fun. You might counter with the argument that insider knowledge deployed in investing in a public stock market is illegal because it confers an unfair advantage on some at the expense of others. You might claim that the owner of a small unquoted company has full insider knowledge and therefore ought to do better investing in his own company. However, consider the following: all managers of all companies have in-depth insider knowledge, yet all companies are not successful and some 70% of young companies fail badly. The insider knowledge is likely to be knowledge of the problems that the company faces, and the value of that is pretty low.

There is a miraculous function that Head Office bean counters perform with great alacrity. Whilst the military lay minefields on the ground, the bean counters lay minefields overhead. One of the ways they do this is to introduce the concept of overhead allocation to the group. The idea is that they allocate head office costs, wherever they can, to operating units, including the cost of time of head office personnel. Extraordinarily expensive systems are devised to get the measurements correct and even then they never reflect the quality of the contribution to the operating unit, only the quantity. And even the quantity is very elusive, especially in relation to the time of senior executives who are not known for their ability to accurately fill in time sheets.

This minefield, laid over the heads of the workers in the field, disables the operating managers. Due to the demotivation caused by heavy charges laid against their performance measurements, charges over which they have no control, they tend to give up. The test of overhead allocation efficacy is for head office personnel to allocate their time to operating units only at the request of the operating unit managers and to agree an outcome and a price before that time is spent. This should demonstrate the quality of the head office interventions. In many companies, this nefarious practice of overhead allocation is used by the parent company as a means of making an expensive top management structure look less costly.

When the number of strategic business units exceeds one, an almost irresistible opportunity comes into play. The logic of realising synergies between the different companies imposes itself in almost a commanding fashion. This opportunity lies under the technical name of 'horizontal strategies' and seeks to find synergies between strategic business units by sharing resources. The outcome proposed is that the overall efficiency of the group will be improved and profits will be greater.

The logic of synergy has certainly been used over and over again to justify takeovers and mergers, from the very largest companies in the world to the very smallest. The truth is that these proposed synergistic benefits are rarely, if ever, realised. Research indicates that 75% of mergers and acquisitions do not realise the benefits. It is probable that in the other 25% the managers, being self-conscious about admitting that they were over-optimistic, are simply covering up the real position. We are talking forced marriages here, ones that will produce an awful lot of arguments later on and, ultimately, divorce.

Synergy is often cited by entrepreneurs as a reason for not allowing strategic business unit to escape and grow. "But they can share part of our warehouse – it's much cheaper" they state emphatically, with a facial expression indicating that the person saying otherwise is completely nuts. They try to make it work, but it fails. It takes the whole group back to the problems of complexity, and the solution to those problems, which was the primary aim of creating the strategic business units in the first place. Now they are stuck, because they have great difficulty publicly admitting that they were wrong.

Sharing resources between strategic business units encourages, and provides an excuse for, corporate management interference. This interference will return the group to the complexity that we set out to eliminate by cutting out the strategic business units. All the old questions will arise: who do we blame when things go wrong? Whose responsibility is it, anyway? Who has the authority to fix it? What resources will we allocate to it?

A better logic to apply is that if there is room in the warehouse for another company's operations, then you have overcapacity and you should get rid of it. Box it off and rent it or take the opportunity to move to a smaller warehouse and cut costs that way. That applies to overcapacity in any area of operations or administration – reduce it, do not share it with another strategic business unit.

The strategic business unit is better off creating contracts with suppliers in the market who are all competing with each other. The strategic business unit then has the power to terminate contracts if the performance by the supplier is inadequate. As the strategic business unit grows, contracts can be renegotiated to take advantage of greater buying power. This advantage is forsaken by trying to exploit synergies between group companies in the form of inter-firm pricing.

Exploiting synergies between strategic business units means that some business units will have to sacrifice some benefit in favour of others. They might have to share a sales force on the grounds that the sales people are calling on the same customers. That has to be cheaper! But what are the effects on performance? With which of the business units do the loyalties of the salespeople lie? If the sales people are carrying a wider range of product, they will understand less about some products than they should do. They are in danger of becoming generalists instead of specialists. Does the customer get confused by the offer?

From the point of view of the managers it will appear that another company is controlling their sales force. You might consider this arrangement as the ideal tool for efficient demotivation! The loyalties of the sales people are split between two business units and they will prefer one over the other, leading to sub-optimal performance.

There will be a loss of autonomy, authority, power and control in the strategic business unit that is forced to participate in this arrangement. Remember, one of the motivational techniques that allow strategic business units to succeed is the autonomy created by cutting out the strategic business units from the parent company. People will always identify more with the strategic business unit that they work for than the group of companies as a whole, because of the local, more cohesive, culture which will form spontaneously. In a small unit the bomber crew bonding will prevail.

Two or more strategic business units working together can gradually become similar, losing their unique differences that are the very ingredients that produce the distinctive capabilities of each strategic business unit. This is the uniqueness that the customers place a high value on when choosing a supplier. These valuable differences are often made up of combinations of people with complementary skills, working together effectively. Breaking up the 'group' and the invisible cohesiveness that you can't define, will destroy the secret ingredient that constitutes the competitive advantage. That is the same competitive advantage that competitors are unable to decipher and copy.

All strategic business units are not the same, so do not be tempted to standardise them. In particular, allow them to grow their own brands. If they share a brand with others, then they will have to be standardised, otherwise the customer will not receive or perceive the consistency of offer that they expect to from a brand. Separate and distinctive brand names will create loyalty and pride amongst the staff. A good brand will also help with recruitment by attracting the right sort of people who already subscribe to the brand values. There is very little advantage in pushing a corporate brand.

One of the major capabilities of strategic business units is their flexibility, in terms of both tactics and strategy. A small company, with a management that is light on its feet, can stay ahead of larger competitors. Being tied to other strategic business units, in any way, will reduce that flexibility and make one or the other, or both, vulnerable to market changes.

In this chapter we talked about cutting out strategic business units that had been created as by-products of the core activities of the main business. The mere fact that they exist indicates that there is a demand for their existence and that the necessary processes to service customers are, at least partly, in place. This is not perfect, but sufficient to indicate that this is a business that has got through its embryonic start-up phases. It is therefore a fairly safe bet for future success compared to a start up from scratch.

Cut out and reform these organically produced businesses as strategic business units first. When you have got used to the practice of owning, but not managing, a bunch of small companies, then you can really have some fun creating some that have not grown directly out of your main business. That is what the next chapter is all about.

Chapter 18

Full Circle

Now that you have cut out all your organically grown strategic business units you can complete the circle and return to creativity. You can start creating businesses all over again – but not exactly in the same way that you did it in the Creative Phase, right at the start of the book.

As Robert Herrick says, "Gather ye rosebuds whilst you may ... tomorrow may be dying" No business lasts forever because markets change, new competitors arrive and new technologies enable new products to be created. Incremental improvements to the typewriter would never have fought back the tide of word processing by computer. You must adopt the strategy of creating new businesses and this must be done whilst the existing businesses are still operating profitably. You cannot stop your business today by, say, selling it off and start a brand new one tomorrow. The momentum would be lost and the whole process would take much longer. And, of course, this second business attempt might fail. There is no strong evidence to indicate that those who sell out and start again have any better success than any first-timer starting their first business.

By the time you reach the 'Divisions In Extended Markets' Phase you are much more experienced in all necessary aspects of business and capable of so much more. As you become experienced and confident in setting up strategic business units, you will find new opportunities become available to you.

You should now be in a position that allows you to create new businesses, new strategic business units, that do not spontaneously arise from your business. Allocate about 10% (rule of thumb) of your annual profits to research and development of the new ideas that might become new business units. Very large companies use corporate management and portfolio management techniques and put 'investment hurdles' in the path of new ventures. Managers have to demonstrate that their idea will generate 20% or so return on internal capital investment, within a relatively short timescale, before they are allowed to proceed. This is nonsense, as you will have realised when you started up. All you can do is go forward and test it and then wait for the return some time in the future.

The level of risk in creating new strategic business units is greater than the risk associated with businesses that have grown organically, within your core company, and then been put out to graze on their own. In general, the further away you go from your knowledge base and what you do in your existing businesses, the greater the risk. Keep your financial investment to a level that you can afford to lose and when you fail, do so gracefully. If you always do what you already do, then you will learn nothing new. Failing gracefully is an essential part of learning. It's a bit like learning to juggle and understanding that, in the early stages when you drop the balls, failure is all part of the process of learning.

Take particular care with marketing spend in new business units. The impatience of managers to grow will lead them to demand large sums of cash for use in foolproof marketing campaigns. Emphasise the need for growth in gross profit before growth in sales. Make sure that the new business goes through all the phases, bearing in mind that it will be quicker than your first start up business because of your experience of the Phases of Growth; except for the Reactive Phase, and that will take just as long. You must allow time in this phase; if you try to move it along by investing heavily in marketing before you have sufficient experience of the new market, you will not develop a satisfying and long-lasting offer. Perversely, fast sales growth in the Reactive Phase can lead you up a cul-de-sac. Equally perversely, immediately after the product launch is the time when the managers will be demanding large sums for marketing. High intensity marketing may initially persuade customers to buy, but if the product has not been honed to produce an exact fit they will switch away to competitors. Read the chapters on the Reactive Phase again.

Your experience of the past will tend to make you think in terms of past recipes. Avoid this at all costs and do so by consultation with your stage hands group, seeking opinions from numerous others. You will need a strong stage hand group at this time and maybe it is the time to recruit some professional non-executive directors. Make sure they put in some useful work in the form of ideas for going forward and controls for preventing unnecessary risk. You will certainly need expert advisers, ones that are capable of understanding strategy, not just impressive names on the headed notepaper. It might also be a good idea if, from your own management team, you supply advisers or non-executive directors to other firms. Teaching and advising are very effective ways of learning, especially if the adviser stays around long enough to see the results of his or her advice.

Use a broad strategic group when creating or developing a new strategic business unit, but always include someone with knowledge of the particular business areas. This might mean including different people: some with knowledge of the new products and market and some with knowledge of the new technologies. You might also need someone with knowledge of the sources of supply.

There are a number of different approaches to creating new strategic business units that now become available to you. For instance, you can form joint ventures with other entrepreneurs. Depending on the nature of your business you may be able to copy the 'Waterman', model whereby your managers become the leader of the new business. Franchising is another option, looked at from the points of view of both the franchisee and the franchisor. Acquisitions, despite the lack of successful examples, are frequently the first thought in the mind of the entrepreneur who wants to create more businesses. Don't go there. An even more risky alternative is starting a company from scratch, introducing new elements (products, technologies, markets etc.) in which you have little or no experience. Each of these options is expanded on in the next few pages. They are approached in the order of risk, starting with the least risky.

Creating joint ventures with partners is a very viable strategic option that is now available to you. But what are the advantages of a joint venture?

For starters, you are sharing the investment with a partner, thereby reducing your financial exposure (as well as limiting your financial rewards). By using partnerships you could start up two companies for the price of one, spreading your business risk.

If you want to extend your markets into new geographical areas or go places with cultural differences, then a partner with local knowledge is worth their weight in silicon chips. They will know where to locate the new centre of operations and where the transport links are. They will know how to employ local personnel and how much they should be paid. They will know how to source efficiently all those essential products and services, such as communication systems, paper clips and lavatory paper and, if they happen to have a few bucks to invest, so much the better. If they do not have a major financial input then you may need two partners – one for local knowledge and another for the investment.

One disadvantage of a joint venture is that there can be some danger in passing on your knowledge, especially if such know-how is strategically important to your other businesses. You could end up by creating a new competitor *and* losing a partner. If you are venturing into a new market, either demographic or geographic, a partnership with someone who knows that market well will allow for much faster penetration of the chosen market. Do it yourself, all on your own, and it could take years longer, thereby allowing more reaction time for your competitors.

If you are thinking about using agents or distributors to penetrate a new market, consider a joint venture as an alternative option. Using a joint venture as the vehicle will allow you a far greater degree of management control. You will be able to influence the pace of growth directly, a process that is difficult with agents and almost impossible with distributors. In addition, it will be easier, with the local knowledge provided by a joint venture partner, to direct (influence) the sales targeting to the best opportunities. Where an agent is used, instead of a joint venture partner, the agent's goal might be to benefit financially by minimising his or her travel costs. The most lucrative, but more distant, customers may be ignored or receive too little attention. Agents and distributors never tell you anything about the market; they view such information as their commercial secrets and, as such, not to be disclosed to anyone else. However, you can judge by the sales volume whether your product is more or less right for the new market

Sometimes, two ordinary resources joined together can create something much greater than the sum of their parts. Once upon a time, I introduced two small firms to each other. One was a graphic designer, creating artwork for brochures and advertisements, and the other a fashion designer, designing and producing up-market, fairly daring clothing. Both were struggling in their respective markets. However, having created a joint venture, they added their talents together and produced a very sexy fashion catalogue that sold at three times the price of a news-stand glossy monthly magazine. This joint venture made more profit than both the partners' separate firms put together!

If you can reproduce, as a joint venture, one of your existing strategic business units within another market (geographic or demographic), then economies of scale can be achieved. A joint venture can more quickly increase the volume of sales, allowing the purchase or manufacture of larger quantities and thereby reducing the unit cost of goods.

In the same way, economies of scope can be realised. Economies of scope refer to anything that has already incurred its costs and yet can be used in other ways without incurring additional costs. For instance, once you have designed a product you have sunk the costs of the design and those costs have been recovered in the price you charge in your existing market. If, however, you now sell the product in a new market you do not have to recover the design costs again. So you can either sell at a lower price, or you can keep your price up and make more profit.

Of course, it is not just from products that you can gain economies of scope. Your brand has cost money to create and maintain. If it can transfer easily to the new market then you will have less cost than if you have to create and build a new brand. But be afraid. Be very, very afraid. Do not try to force an existing brand into a new market just to save on costs. Make sure that it is a good fit and then expect to tweak it a little bit, or a big bit. I'm always a little nervous when companies engage in brand dilution.

In allowing different strategic business units to trade, take care that you do not end up with a 'let's exploit group synergies' situation. Treat any inter-company trading as fully commercial transactions.

If you import stuff for your existing businesses and you have to pay for that stuff in a foreign currency, you will expose yourself to a foreign currency risk. You can reduce or eliminate that risk if you have a source of revenue in the same foreign currency. If you create a joint venture in the foreign country that you already buy from and generate sales revenue in the local currency, then you will be able to pay for your imports in the same currency. Voila! The foreign exchange risk has vanished.

Exploit the cultural differences between your different markets, not only differences arising from geography, but also from customer behaviour within market segments. Pizza comes from Italy, but an American pizza or a British pizza is distinctly different from an Italian pizza, Eminem isn't black, but he raps. By combining cultural features from different markets you may be able to create combinations of desirable factors that are unique. Desirable uniqueness is where the most profitable price is, and that is where you want to be.

A joint venture can yield value if you want to venture into an area where you need to gain knowledge of a new technology and you find a potential partner who already has the expertise at their disposal. You may even be able to access a source of supplies, otherwise unavailable to you, through a joint venture.

In the management of a joint venture, always treat it as a strategic business unit, with its own management team who have both responsibility and authority. Whilst there should be trust between the joint venture partners, do not confuse trust with naiveté. My personal experience indicates that few such alliances are free from hidden agendas and some skulduggery.

A British firm formed a joint venture with a firm in another European country, which country hosted the joint venture operation. It took a couple of years before the British firm became aware of a little skulduggery. The local management of the joint venture partner company, whenever they ran short of cash, diverted some from the joint venture bank account into their own bank account. Not major theft in the legal sense, as they paid it back, but dangerous for the joint venture partner. If the borrower had been forced into liquidation before the borrowings could be repaid…

Most joint ventures break up after a few years and sometimes even more quickly. Define a divorce mechanism, a pre-nuptial agreement, before you enter into the joint venture. Beware of giving away your *strategic* resources and capabilities to your partner because partners commonly re-emerge as competitors. As a partner in a joint venture, behave like a student, not like a teacher. Ask the question of yourself, frequently: "What are the logical future implications if both parties behave in their own best interest?"

The second major and low risk opportunity for creating new strategic business units is the 'Waterman' model. If you employ highly skilled or professional workers or managers you will find that, at some point in their career, they feel they ought to strike out on their own and have a shot at creating and building their own business. I have seen some entrepreneurs become quite upset when they have discovered a manager preparing to jump overboard, lured by the song of the Sirens on the island of Ionabusiness. The entrepreneur tries to keep the manager tied to the mast by appeals to their loyalty, "When you came to me, son, you were nothing but a deckhand, and just look at you now" When that fails, the warnings are issued, "You'll never make it on your own. You'll be begging for your old job back".

So, when the skilled professional plans on leaving your company, do the decent thing. Go with them. I do not mean giving up everything else and walking into the sunset, holding hands. What I mean is, offer them investment and other help and guidance, in setting up their own operation. In return for your money and your time, take a sizeable, but minority stake in their business. Never, ever take a majority stake; it is their business and must remain so in order to motivate them. However, do encourage them from time to time to take in another shareholder or two so that the shares become more liquid and therefore more easily bought and sold. You might want to exit, with cash in place of the shares, sometime in the future.

Depending on the nature of the business, the Waterman model can create an informal 'bench' of sub-contractors who will prove to be loyal and dependable. For instance, a software development company handles the escapee, not by taking shares in his or her business, but by sub-contracting work to them from time to time. This helps the main company manage the fluctuations in market demand. The sub-contractors remain loyal because, in their mind, the main company takes the form of an insurance policy, covering their risk of unemployment in the future.

The third option for creating new strategic business units is franchising. Here we deal only with the 'business format' type of franchise, leaving the other methods of franchising and licensing to other authors.

People who work in businesses tend to associate franchising with people who are naïve in business matters and who need a ready-made business, with masses of support, in order to succeed. Most people who own and run businesses think only in terms of being a franchisor. But it can be extremely profitable for a big, grown-up businessman to become a franchisee.

In such cases it may be possible to negotiate some good deals with the franchisor. Once, when leading a turnaround in a rag trade retail group, I focused on developing a chain of Benetton franchises which turned out to be the most profitable of the three divisions in the company. It was astonishingly simple to accomplish and took up very little senior management time. Strictly speaking, describing a franchise as a *strategic* business unit is not entirely accurate, as the franchisor has already decided on virtually all the strategies.

Obtaining the head franchise rights of a global brand for an entire country can be beneficial and is very similar to the previous example. Except that you will be selling franchises instead of buying them. You can, of course, keep a few franchises and operate them yourself, thereby keeping close to the market. The development work on the business format has been done and the remaining tasks for the head franchisee is finding franchisees, supervising their operation and providing the predetermined support, such as marketing promotion.

Would any of your businesses be suitable to be franchised, with you as the franchisor? You could build a global empire very rapidly based on a viable franchise. Bear in mind that franchising is an operations technology that straddles both distribution technology and geographical area. If you are not experienced in these elements of the business then you will have to buy in the skills.

Do not underestimate the amount of work involved in creating a franchise operation. Developing the pilot ventures, which are necessary to validate the concept so that you can prove it to others, will take a considerable length of time. Would you buy into a franchise where the pilot had only been operating for nine months? Similarly, developing the operating manual will take a long time. Developing the manual is similar to going through the Reactive Phase, the Processes Phase and the Empowerment Phase of a start-up company. However, once systematised it needs only to receive the attention of the Cybernauts, when feedback dictates.

Your efforts do not stop there. You must define the type of franchisees that you want and then you must find and attempt to sell them a franchise. Then you will have to find the locations that fit with your corporate image. Both these tasks are ongoing, throughout the entire life of the franchise operation.

The fourth option for creating new strategic business units is the acquisition of existing companies. Research indicates that business acquisitions by large corporates take about eight years on average to produce an adequate return.

The problem is inherent in the acquisition of established businesses that come covered in the porcupine spines of their own unique culture; they need careful handling. Managers of the acquiring company seem to invariably underestimate both the problems of integration in relation to culture clash and to the time it takes to adjust. When one company gobbles up another company it may take several years to digest. Meanwhile, there is a lot of painful heartburn, which may be felt by the customers as well as the employees.

The 'eight years to return' problem is largely a reflection of the unrealistic profit expectations of corporate managers, who are not fully aware of the necessary trade-off of profits against growth. If you re-invest your profits you will grow faster, but show lower profits. If you declare profits and pay tax on them, you will grow more slowly. When you already have a stable of existing strategic business units you can afford to be patient. You may not have to be as patient as eight years, especially if you do not subject the new acquisitions to portfolio management and horizontal strategies.

You can expand your empire by acquiring ready-made businesses, but you will be faced with cultural differences that you may never be able to sort out. In most cases, you will find that the management that came with the new business will not convert to your way of thinking and, within a short time, either they will leave or you will squeeze them out. People will always identify more with the strategic business unit they work for than the group of companies as a whole. This is particularly evident where the strategic business unit has been bought-in and has a different history from the rest of the company. Think carefully about acquisitions before you make an offer to buy. "What is it, exactly, that I'm buying?" you might ask yourself. Perhaps a bunch of customers that you could have switched to your own operation, had you started up as a competitor?

Maybe you just bought an idea. Well, ideas are cheap, two a penny, and ideas do not make money. First class implementation is what makes the money. Leonardo Da Vinci: nice helicopter, poor implementation.

Usually, the only thing worth buying is a motivated manager who could perform as a managing director. Do not grow by acquisition – it's usually just a silly piece of machismo. If you can't beat them in a straightforward competition, then you are not good enough to be in that business, anyway.

The acquisition that will really work for you is the one where the guy who had the idea is also the managing director and has a need for some moral support and shelter. His company is a very tiny embryo, maybe five people altogether, and has been going less than two years. Treat him in the same way as any other managing director of a business unit. Buy him in, rather than buy him out, and reward him with a large share of the business. This guy is going to astonish you with his commitment and determination to succeed. And he probably will succeed, if his idea is any good. If his idea is crap, then you've got yourself a very valuable and enthusiastic manager who will almost bite your hand off when you offer him a position as managing director of another business. By the way, you don't usually have to look very far for these guys.

There is a possible exception to the acquisitions advice as set out previously and that is in the case of 'turnarounds'. When a company is in deep trouble and you can see how to cure their illness, then you might consider them. Usually, there is a crisis situation and the jobs of all the managers and staff are in jeopardy. In such a crisis, the existing culture loses its cohesive qualities and everybody becomes amenable to change. A crisis also means that people will tolerate an autocratic management style, which means that you can move fast to achieve the turnaround.

You will, of course, need to be familiar with the techniques of turnarounds or to have, or be able to bring in, a turnaround specialist. It is extremely demanding to engage in a turnaround and it will need a 100% degree of focus on the task by the turnaround manager. Frequently, the first three months or so are referred to as 'the 100 days rage', and it really does feel like suppressed and controlled rage.

Companies that need a turnaround can be relatively low risk, if you can buy them cheaply enough. I know asset strippers get a bad press, but be alert to the possibility that they have undervalued assets. If assets are undervalued or underutilised it reflects badly not only on the company managers, but it also has an adverse effect on the whole economy. Every time there is inefficient use of assets, it makes someone poorer than they would otherwise be; conversely, any gain in efficiency creates wealth for the world.

The fifth, and most risky, option for creating new strategic business units is to create them from scratch. In the previous chapter we discussed the elements that make up a business. We did so in the context of analysing the company in order to locate the organic businesses that had grown within the company. We defined these businesses in order to separate them out and reduce the complexity of the whole company. The elements were: product, market, operating technology, distribution technology and geographic area. We mentioned that sourcing might be considered to be an element, as well.

Now we can make use of these elements again in order to produce new business units. Create a card for each product or service supplied by each of the existing businesses – this constitutes the product pack. On separate cards, write the markets that each business unit trades into, thereby creating the market pack. Bear in mind that these markets might be divisible into distinct customer segments.

Produce more cards for the operating technologies used by each business and for their distribution technology or process. Do likewise for the geographical areas in which each business operates and for the sources of supply.

We now have packs of cards that include all the elements of business that you know well. Now set up an all-night card game, with plenty of beer and sandwiches, and shuffle the separate packs. Take one card from each pack and combine them into a business. Most of the results will be absolute rubbish, but you just might come up with a brilliant new business formula. However, after a while you will come to know all the cards and your mind will start combining elements, without the need for the cards. You are now into brainstorming within your own brain, but you have set parameters – the elements of the businesses in which you already have experience. Any businesses that you produce in this way are more risky than the organically grown strategic businesses, but less risky than pure diversification, by which I mean engaging with elements of which you have no experience.

You can gradually introduce new elements. If your existing businesses only distribute through wholesalers, why not distribute through retailers? Or direct to consumers? If you do not make much use of the Internet, can you apply this technology to any of your markets or products? If you only manufacture in-house, consider outsourcing. Take an existing business and change just one element and you have a new business. Or change two elements, which will increase the level of risk.

When you are considering markets include a consideration of segmentation which goes beyond conventional demographics. For instance, sourcing includes country of origin benefits. Many consumers, practising gourmets, gourmands, Epicureans and Sybarites buy cheeses and wines because the source of the product is France. Some people will be happy to buy German engineered products, but hesitate to buy engineering from other countries. As we saw when we explored the differences between high street book retailers and Amazon, markets can be segmented by the customers preferring different methods of selection or distribution.

You do not have to diversify very far in order to produce viable new businesses. Just as well, because diversification is extremely risky when you start using elements of which you have no experience.

The business units that you have created will grow-up and accumulate little organic growths within themselves – another source of free businesses that you do not have to acquire at great cost.

What can you do with dozens of business units, how can you cope?" The answer – sell them.

Sell them to their management teams as 'management-buy-outs' and, if you think it might pay off, keep a bit for yourself. Be aware that, if the managers know that they are going to be allowed to buy out their strategic business unit, strange orchestral manoeuvres in the dark may commence. The managers may start to deliberately underperform, thereby reducing the price of the company. After they own the company they will return to their normal and better levels of performance.

Sell them to managers outside the business by using the process of 'management-buy-ins'. Keep in touch with the venture capitalists that create and finance such teams. With the team coming from outside, this process leaves you less open to 'moral hazard', meaning mischief, by your managers.

When you have created many strategic business units, here are a few extra pointers. Take care not to manage the strategic business units as they can do that for themselves. Here's a real-life example: the boss of the group went off to become chairman of the local football club and enjoyed it so much that he forgot about his empire of half a dozen companies. Profits went up to record levels everywhere in the group of companies. Whilst juggling, if you focus on the balls, you will drop them; focus beyond them, see them only in peripheral vision and they will stay moving in perfect rhythm.

Insist that the managers listen to advice from several members of the stage hands group, even if they do not always take it and apply it. Take care to motivate any advisers – a 1% shareholding in a business unit with a planned exit route can produce an extraordinary amount of activity in an adviser. An accountant, external to a company that I know well, had a tiny percentage of the shares and realised a cash sum after holding them for four years. If he had charged all the time he spent working for free for the company, it would have come to just about the amount he received on exit. It seems that there is more motivational power in a shareholding than just monetary value.

Allow for selling off a business unit every now and again. If the managing director of the strategic business unit makes a small fortune in the process, then publicise it widely, in as much detail as is legally possible (buyers frequently do not want the price paid to become common knowledge). It demonstrates to your remaining managing directors that it pays handsomely to remain loyal and see the job through to the end. It also encourages other aspiring entrepreneurial managing directors to apply to be brought into your kingdom. The structure that you have now created is somewhat similar to that in which a medieval king and his barons co-existed.

The central problem troubling King John arose from his management of the barons. Military rebellion always appeared to be just round the corner. King John's ever-increasing taxation of the barons was a major cause of resentment, as he took more and more from them to finance investments in ill-fated ventures abroad. This practice is exactly the same as the portfolio management practice of relieving business units of their surplus cash and redirecting the funds to other business ventures. If you want to go on a crusade do not rook your barons in order to do so. If you feel the need to build a war chest from the cash flow of the business units – do not do so.

Avoid favouritism, like the plague. Favouritism in dealing with the barons caused a great deal of trouble for King John and is still a recognised problem in the field of leadership studies. It results in the formation of an 'in-group' and an 'out-group'; that was exactly the King's problem, and this phenomenon appears in an identical form in today's business world. The 'in-group' gets more of the King's resources, more of his time and more information. The confidence of the 'in-group' is strengthened by the King's concern for it, and consequently it tends to perform better than the 'out-group', which becomes jealous and rebellious. It's a vicious spiral of decline.

Another of King John's problems was that the barons were resentful of being forced to provide services to the King, such as supplies and men for his military adventures in France. This resentment was exacerbated by the public failures of the King's ventures. Notice the similarity to the failure of horizontal strategies.

The King and the barons have fundamentally the same interest in maintaining the social order. In the case of King John, his barons created a list of demands and backed it up by a show of military strength. They forced him into negotiations until he finally came up with the Magna Carta charter of rights, which largely satisfied the barons and gave King John a thing or two, as well.

It's far better for you to anticipate these problems and produce easy-to-agree charters of your own. Contracts of employment provide the vehicle for the legal relationships with the managing directors of the businesses and shareholders agreements are a perfect place for setting out the rules of the game for those who own part of the business. You will always get the occasional rogue baron and you should remember to include the means of getting rid of them in your 'charters'. Consider, where appropriate, fixed-term contracts, renewable only if both parties agree.

When King John died, he left behind an extraordinarily competent bunch of barons who remained loyal to future Angevin kings. Not a bad epitaph.

Chapter 19

Finally…

…I experienced a huge amount of enjoyment and satisfaction in writing this book and I fervently hope that you, the reader also enjoyed it, and will be of a mind to start your own company.

The intention of this book is to inspire you to grow your own company. If you do so, you could grow rich, satisfy your creative urges and make a significant contribution to the society in which you live.

For some reason, unknown to me, those men and women who have gone through business school and emerged with an MBA tend not to start their own growth companies. There are exceptions, of course. I have worked with several MBAs, most of whom were successful, including some that turned their efforts into millions. Only one failed to achieve the Delegation Phase and was satisfied running a small company that paid him a reasonable salary. My sample is too small to be statistically significant, but it is likely that MBAs have a greater chance of creating a successful company, compared to non-MBAs. There is some evidence from the USA that those who have work experience and an MBA are the most likely people to create their own successful growth company.

If you were to fail, just get a notebook, sit down in a coffee shop and start again. I suggest a coffee shop rather than your desk at home, because there are more opportunities to react to people. Get used to talking with strangers – tell them that you are starting a company. Ask them for help – you'll be amazed by the positive contribution that they will make. Should you interact with some downbeat characters that warn you of pitfalls – listen to them, too.

When you get close to the year of your retirement and you look back over your life to examine what you did with it, do you want to conclude: "I worked for a big company and did my very best for them".

Throughout this book I have emphasised that the entrepreneur must stay close to the customer, who is the final arbiter of the performance of the company. This is, first and foremost, the most important factor in growing a company and should be carried through all the Phases of Growth.

Remember that the Phases can overlap and that they recur throughout the life of the company. When you want to introduce a new product to the market, then revert to the Creative and Analysis Phases. You will need monitor the progress of the new product and react to the market – the Reactive Phase.

If the systems that are needed to support the new product differ from your other products, you must enter Processes Phase again. And, if you appoint a manager for the new product, you will enter the Empowerment Phase again.

The second most important factor in creating a successful growth company is the structure of the company. It must be the money-making machine. Why? Because it has scalability – it needs only one creative act, followed by reproduction.

If you are working as a consultant or as a designer each creative production will be unique; each job that you do will be different and scalability is limited. It is very difficult to grow, when each job is *ad hoc* – you can do so only by adding more production people. Whilst you might make a good living, you will be working hard forever. In contrast, the money-making machine is simply replicating one or more products and, because you can easily delegate the processes, there is no intrinsic limit to growth. Consequently, whilst earning a good salary, you can grow a company into a saleable asset which will sell for millions.

A last thought: if you happen to be an advisor to growing companies, then you need to familiarise yourself with all the Phases of Growth, to the extent that you can diagnose what Phase the company IS in and advise appropriately.

Thank for reading this book.